Meditative Mandala Menagerie

An Advanced Coloring Book

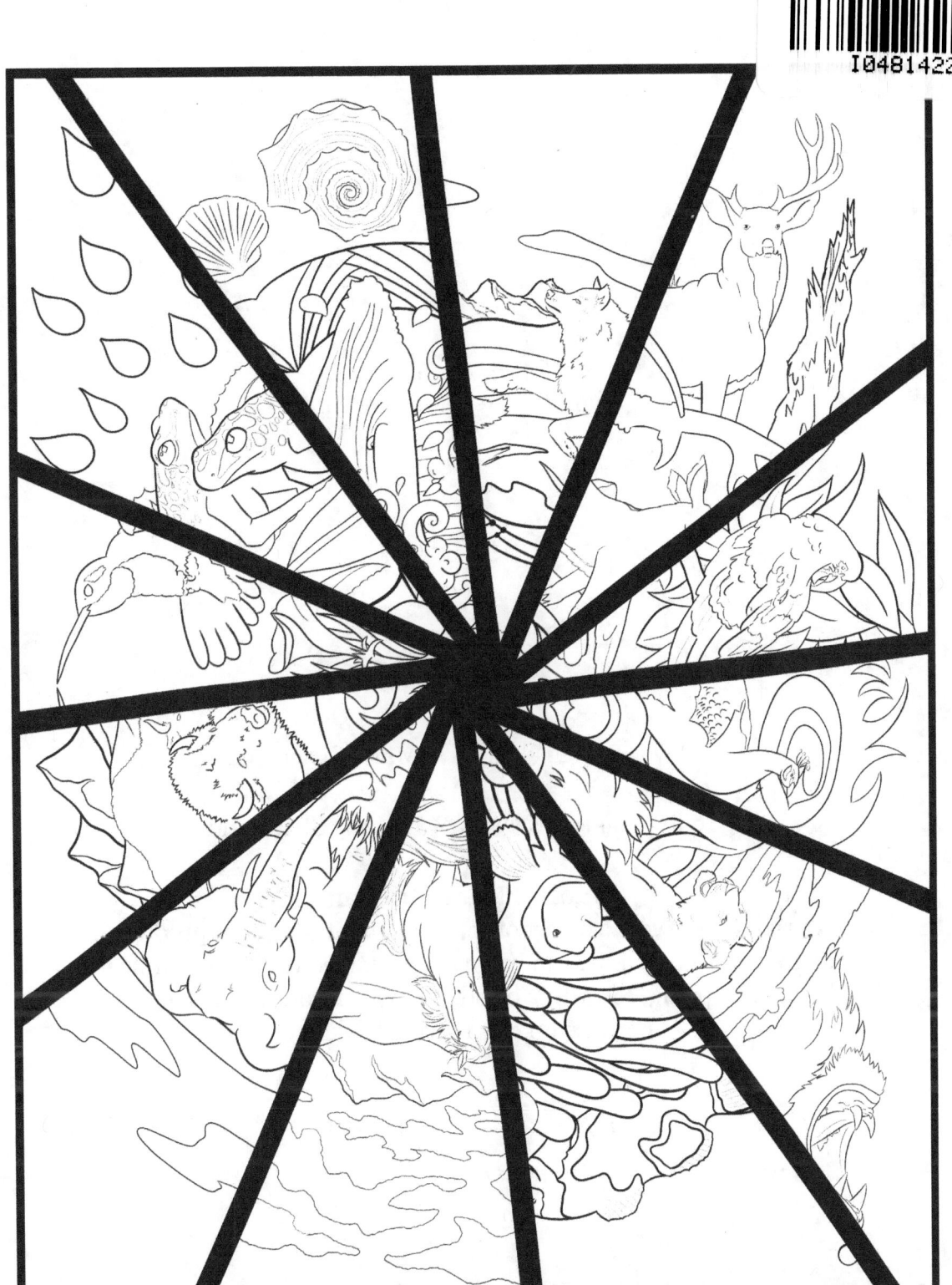

J. Marie Strickland

J.Marie Strickland
paintingsbyjms@mail.com

ISBN-10: 1983570532
ISBN-13: 978-1983570537

Hello coloring enthusiast!

Welcome to the *Meditative Mandala Menagerie*. Inside you'll find 30 coloring pages with animals and landscapes worked into mandalas for an advanced, meditative coloring experience. Some are more complex than others, for a widely varied and enjoyable coloring experience, no matter what you're in the mood to tackle.

Each image will be followed by a blank page, so you are free to cut out your pages, hang them without sacrificing another coloring page; and also to allow you to control bleed through. If you are coloring with markers I highly recommend placing a blank paper between your current page and the page following.

I hope you enjoy coloring them as much as I enjoyed drawing them and coloring them myself.

Happy coloring!

J.Marie Strickland

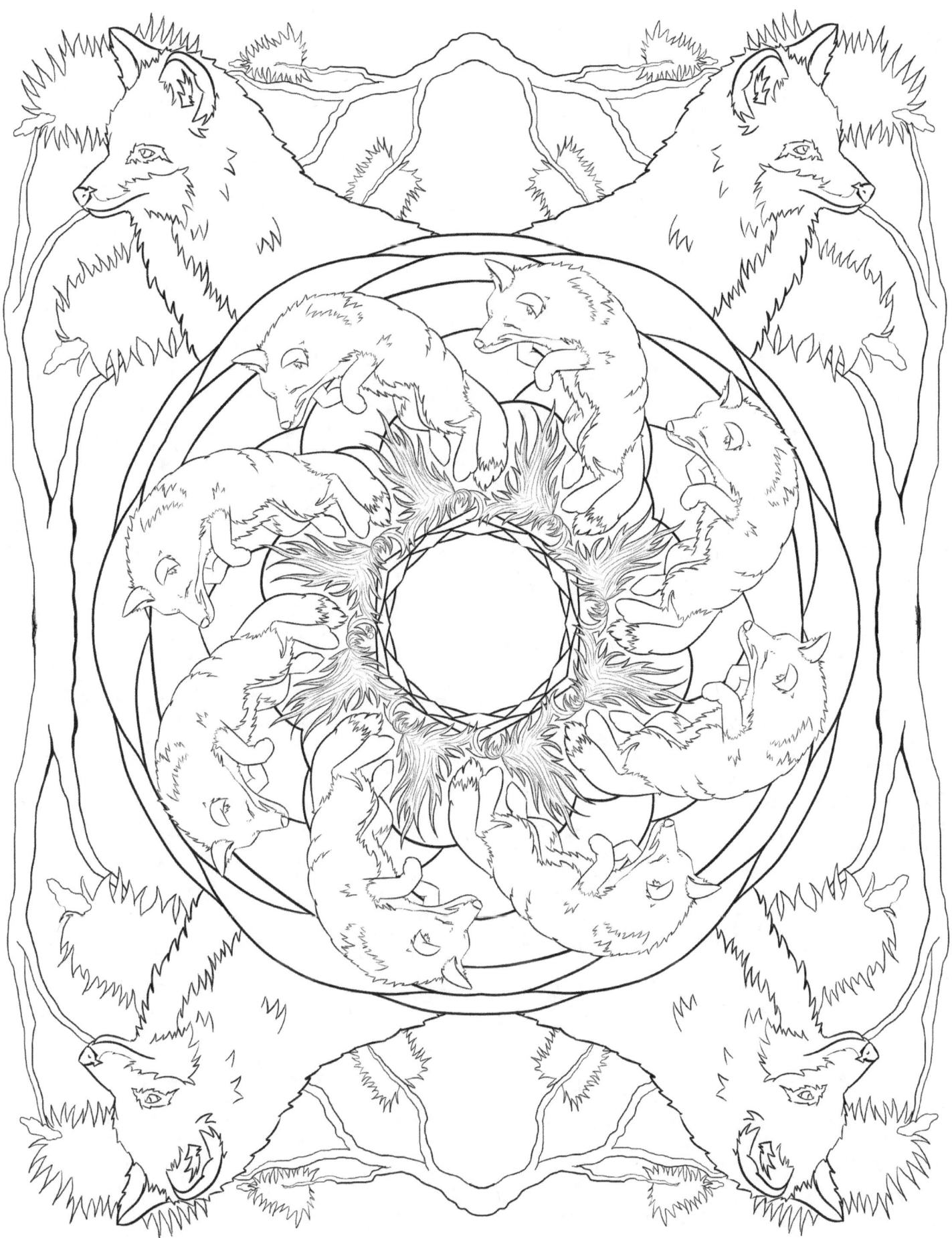

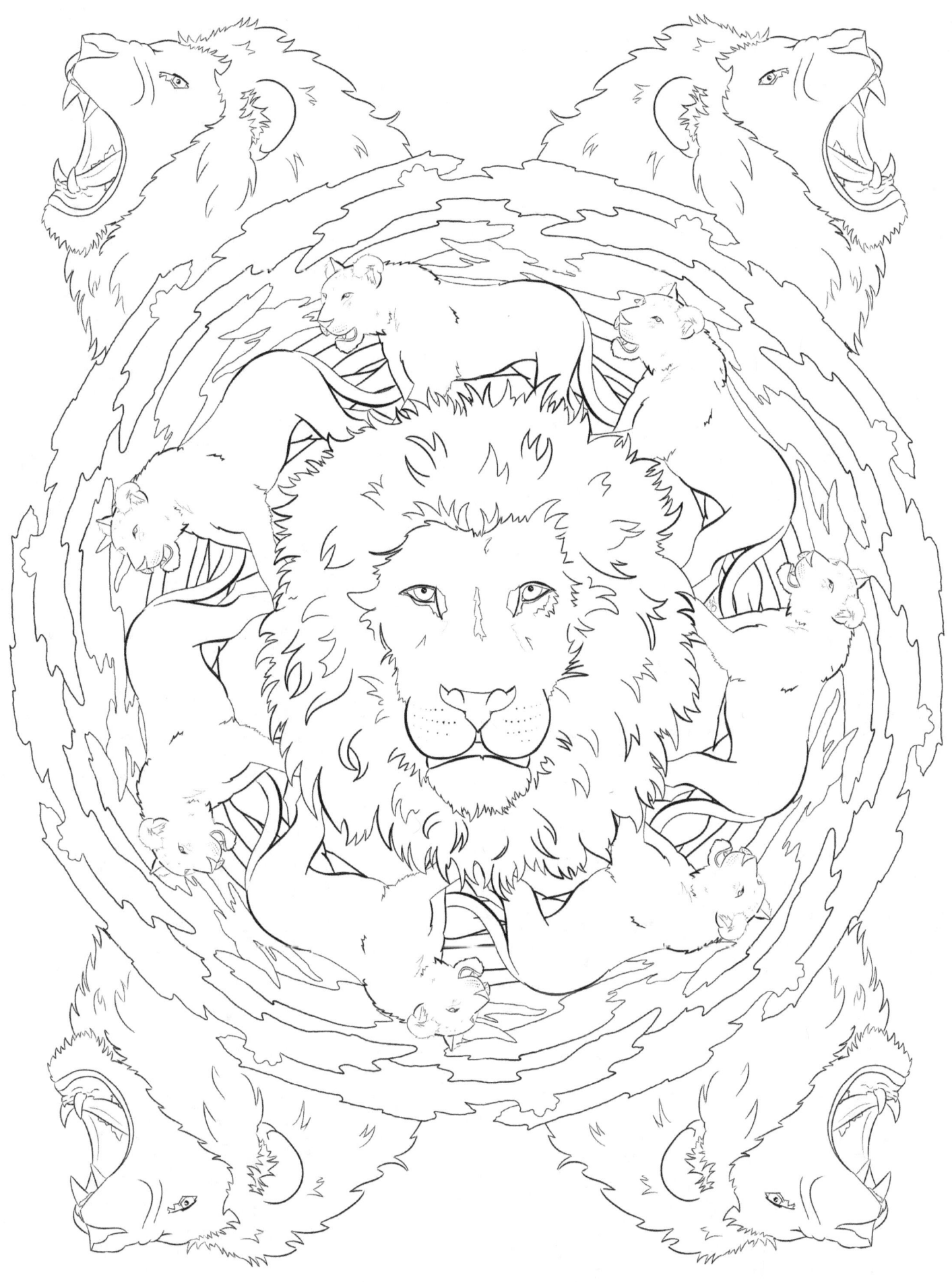

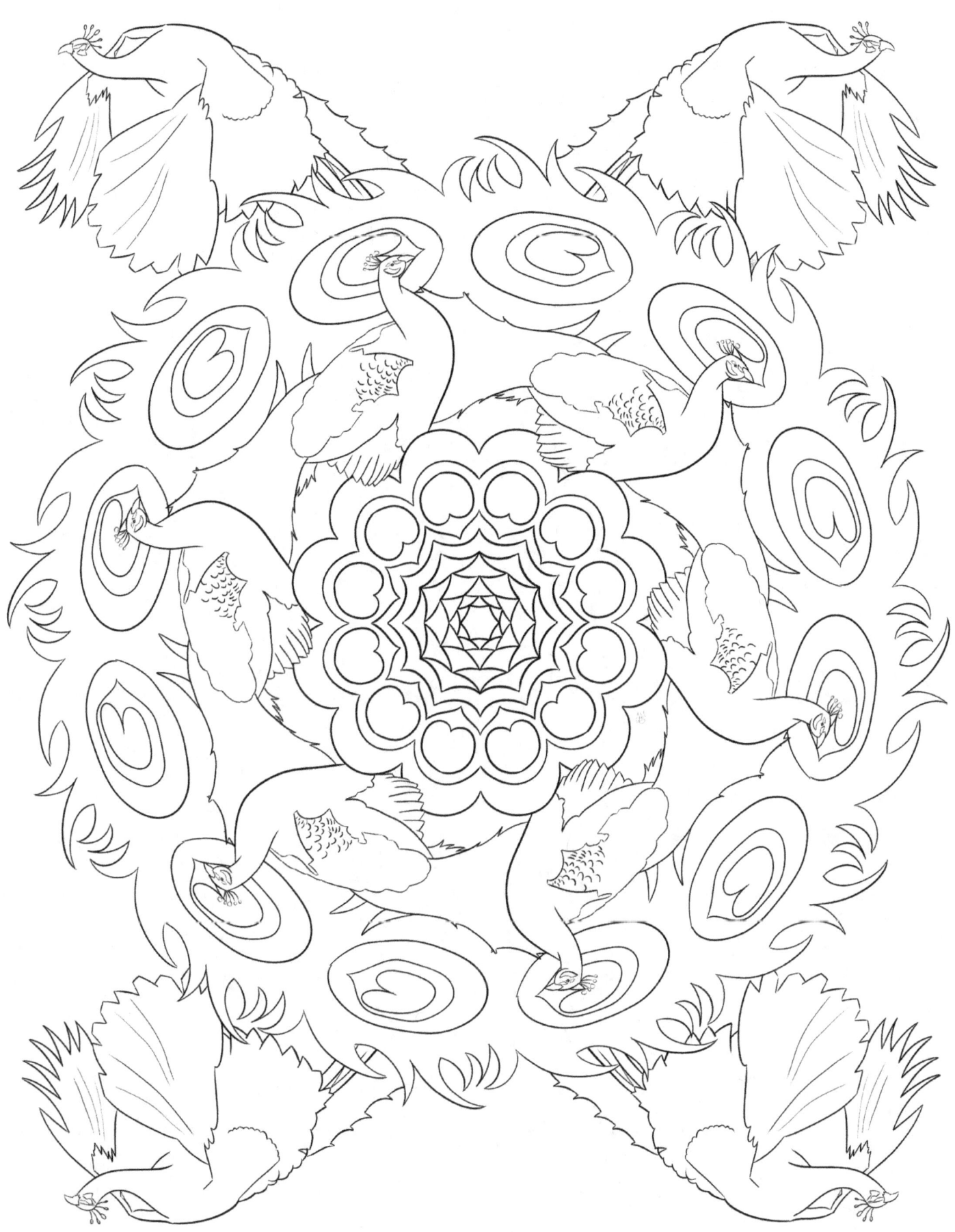

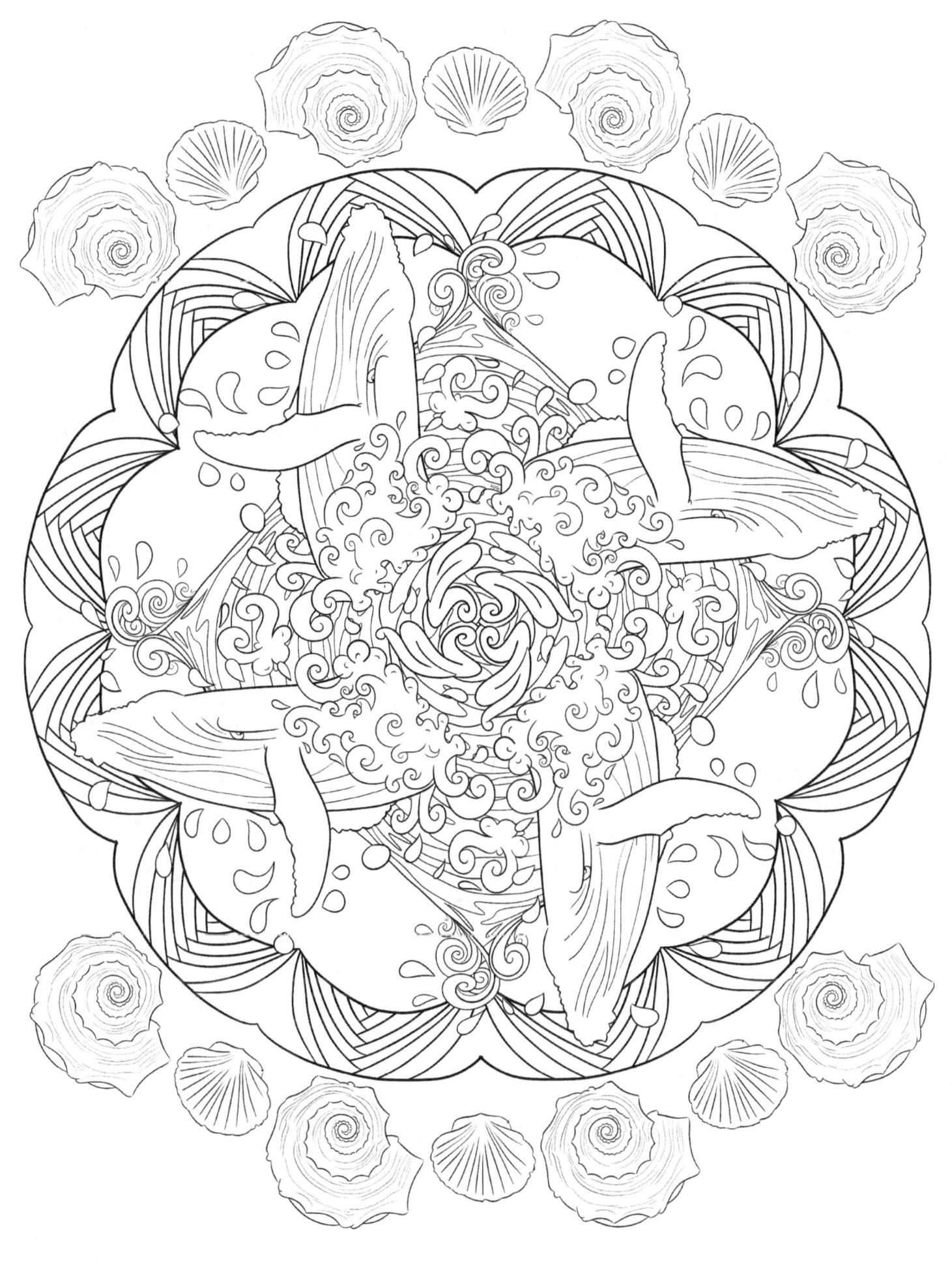

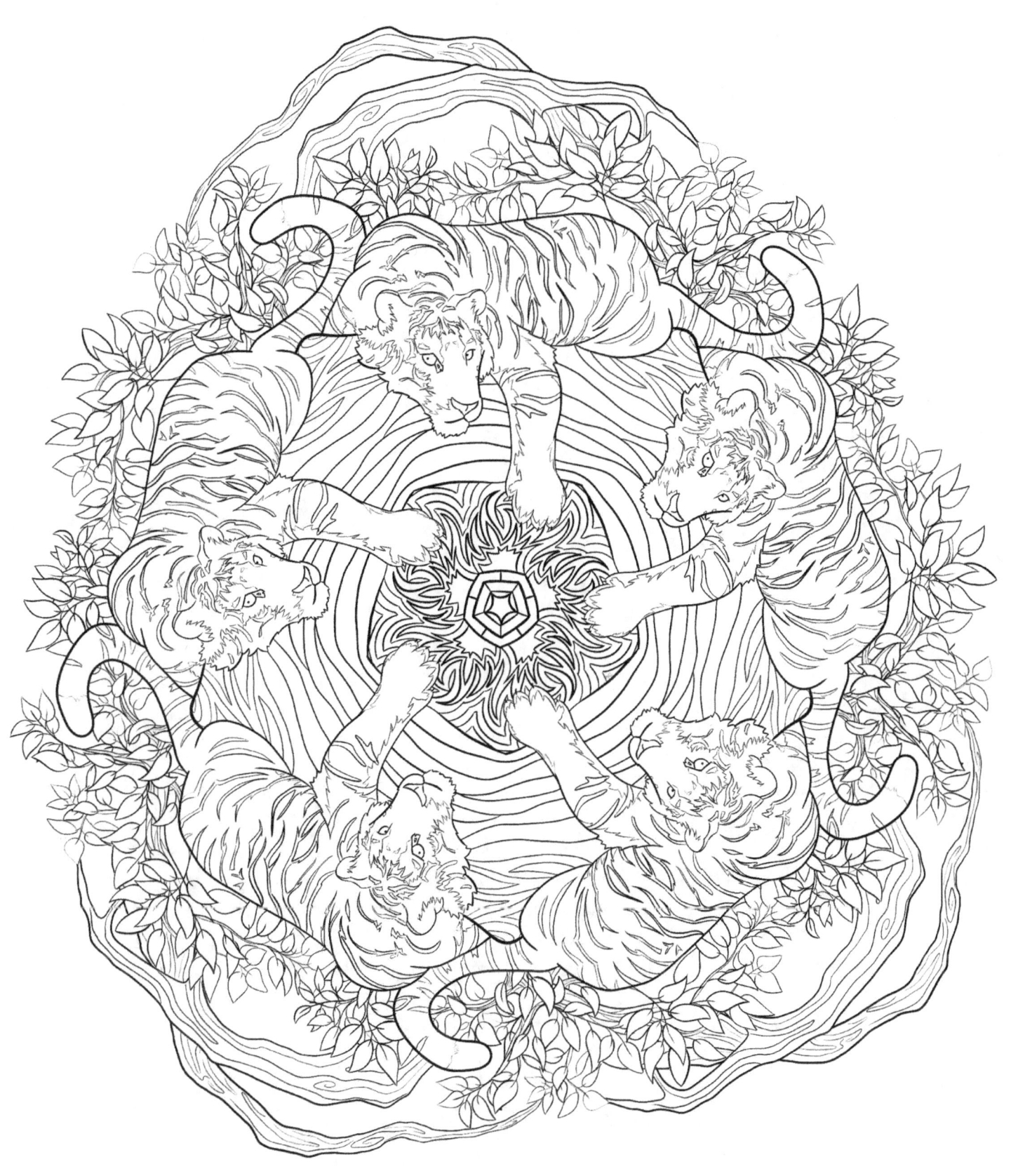

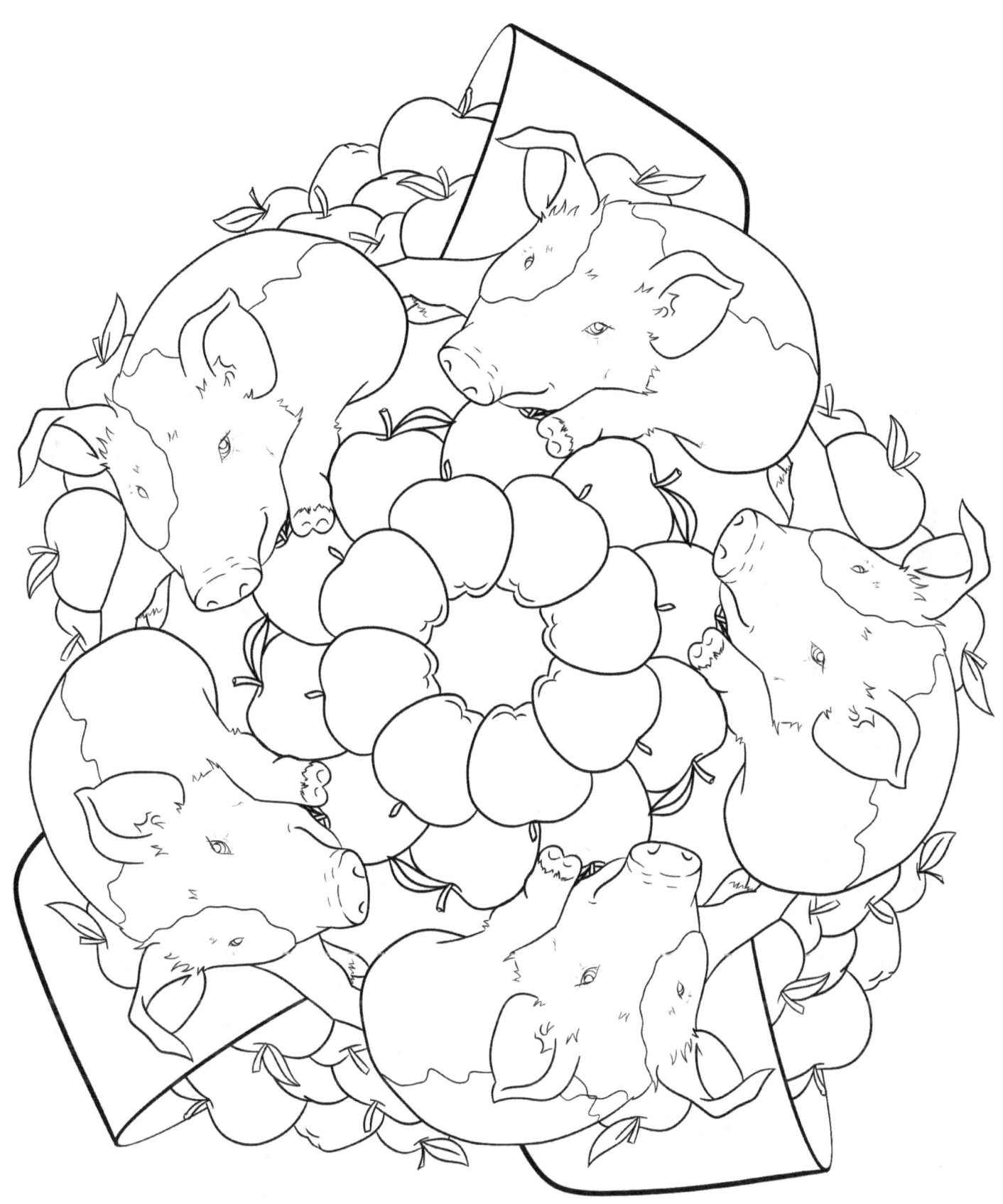

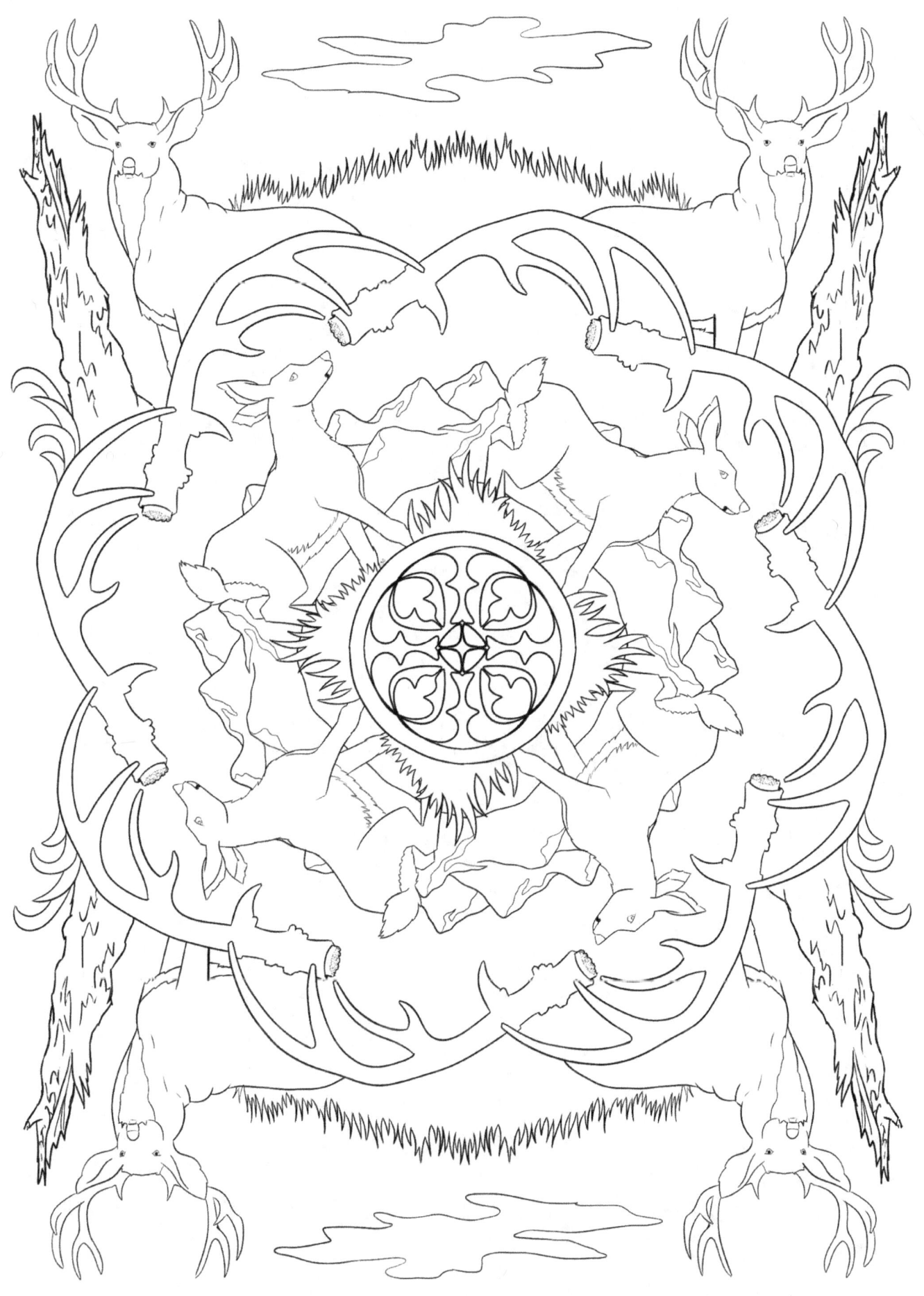

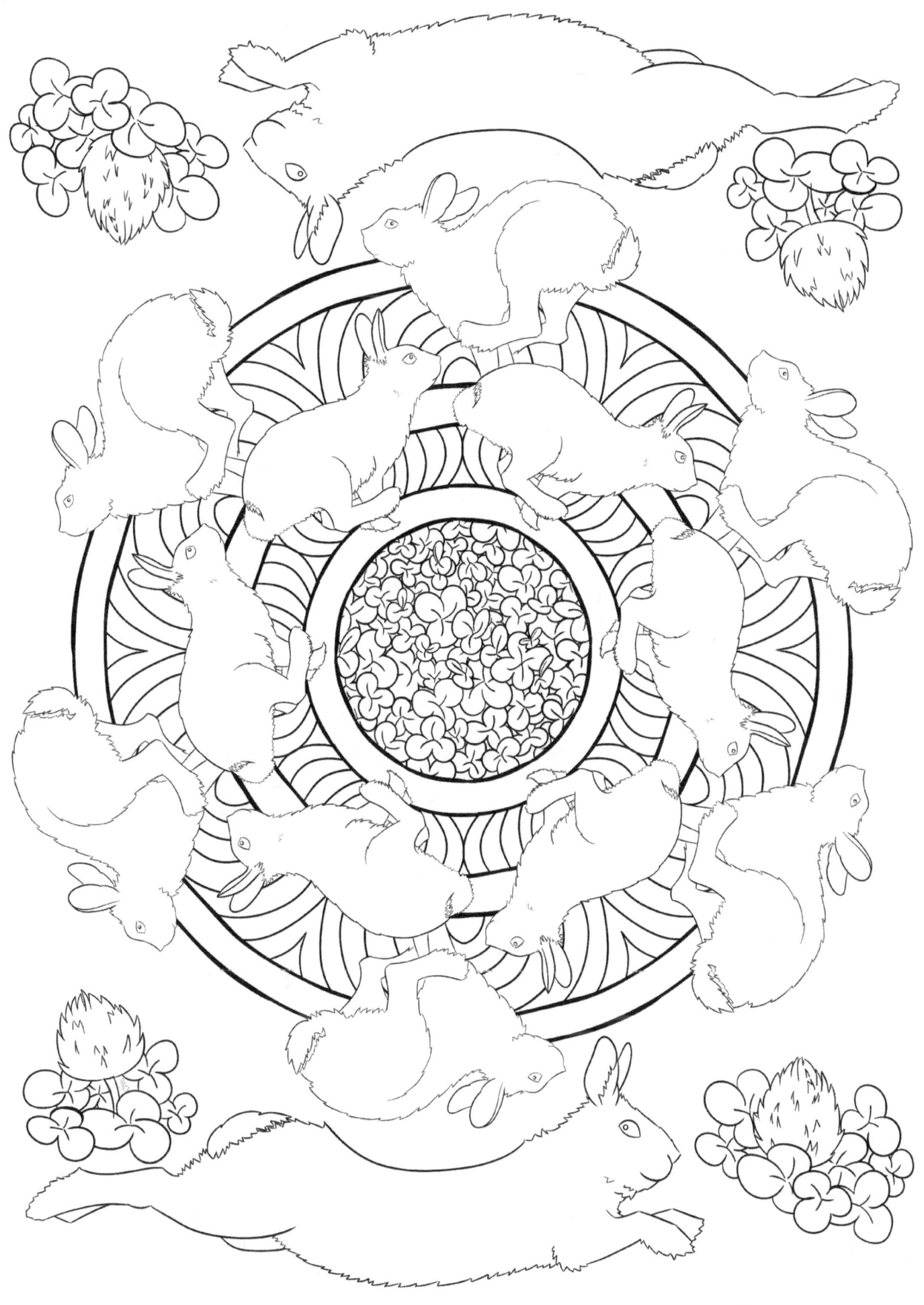

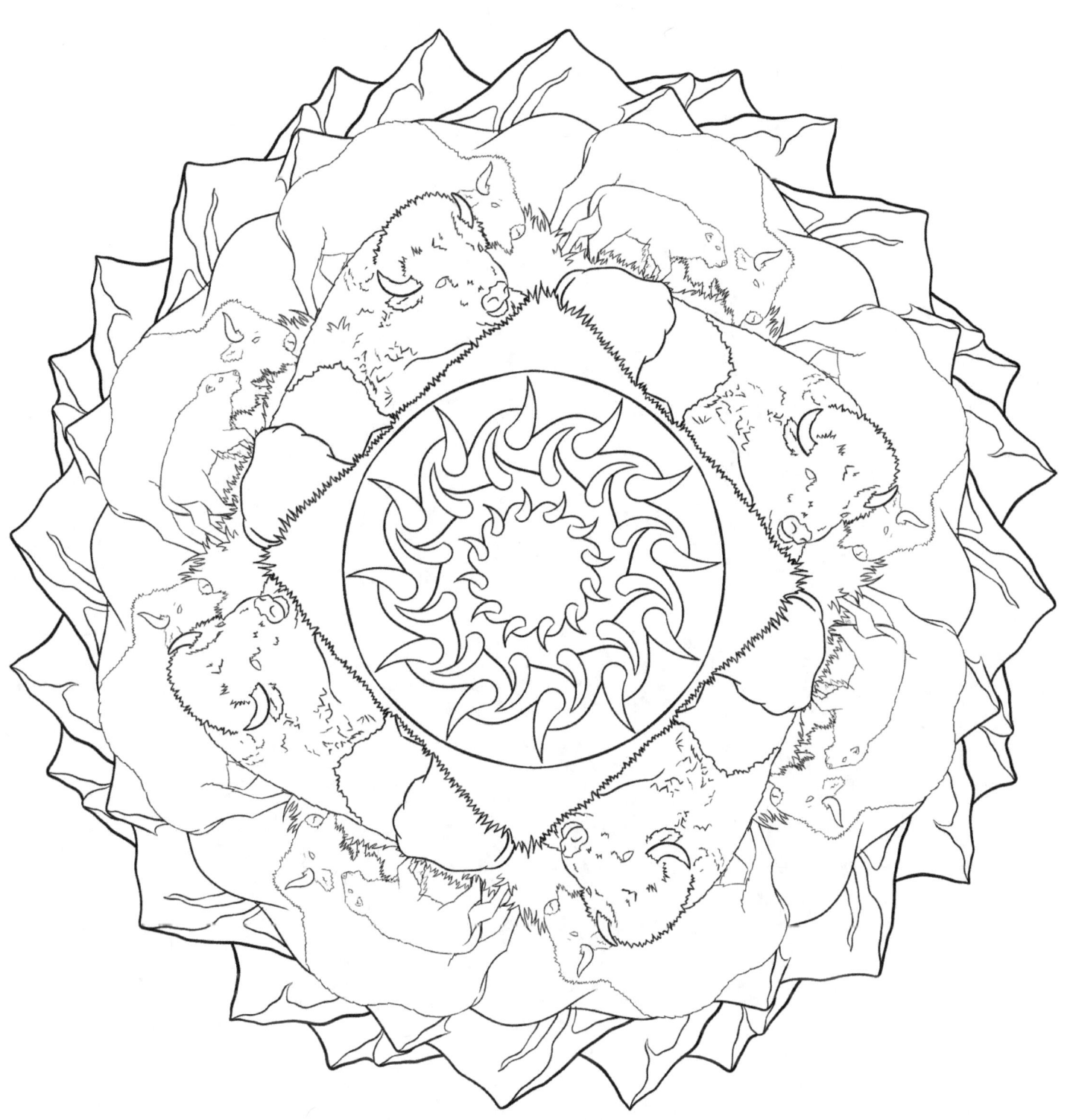

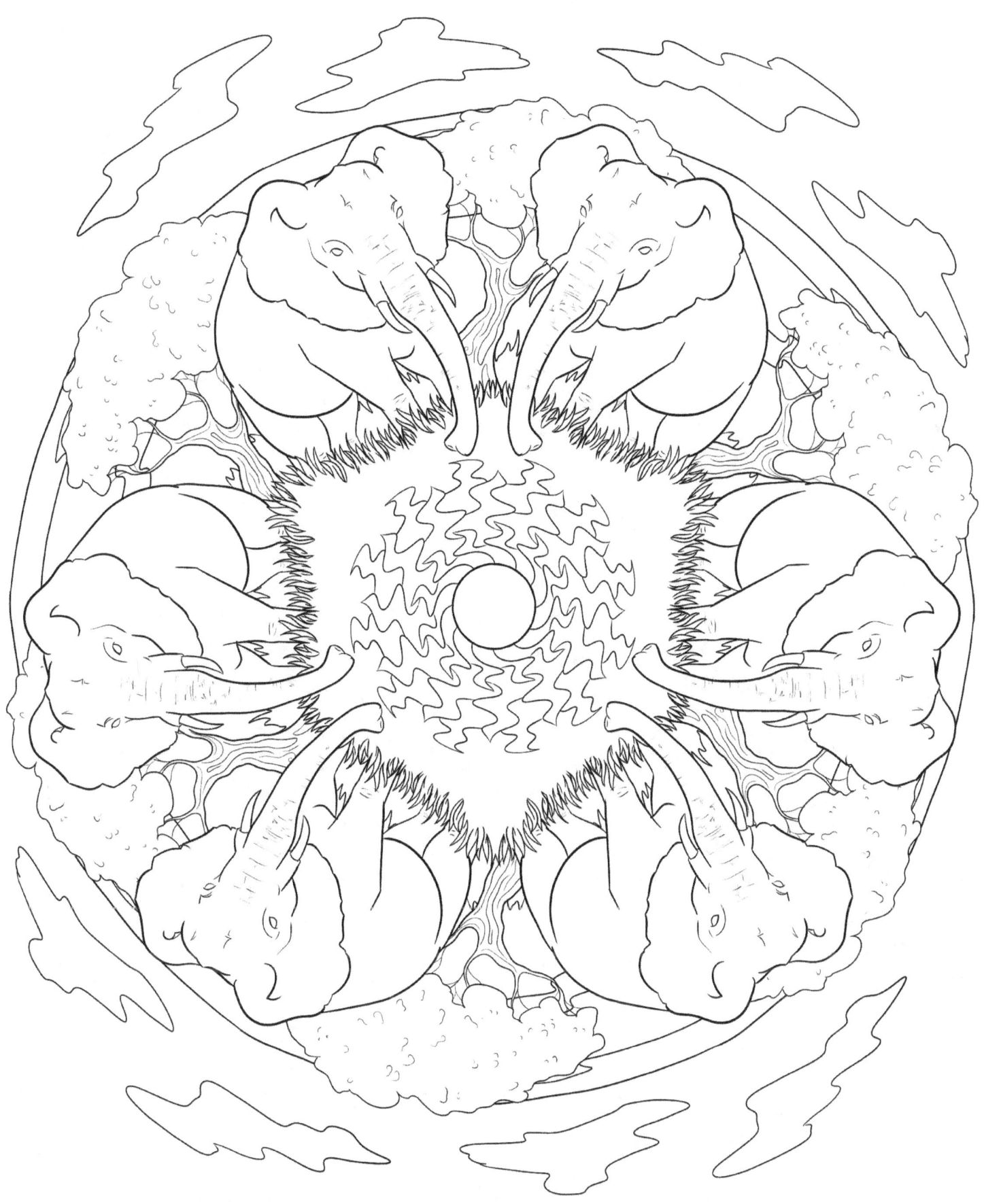

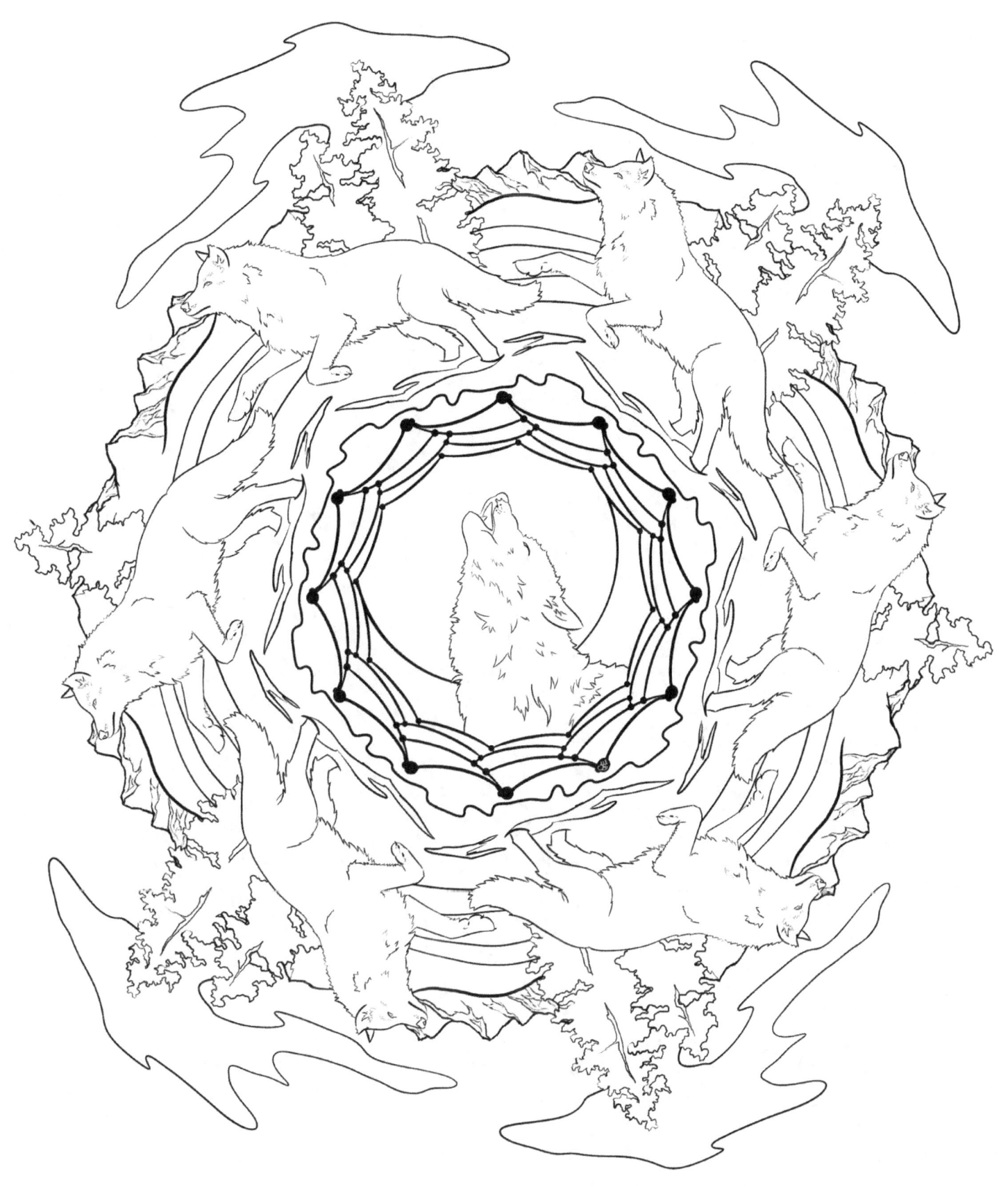

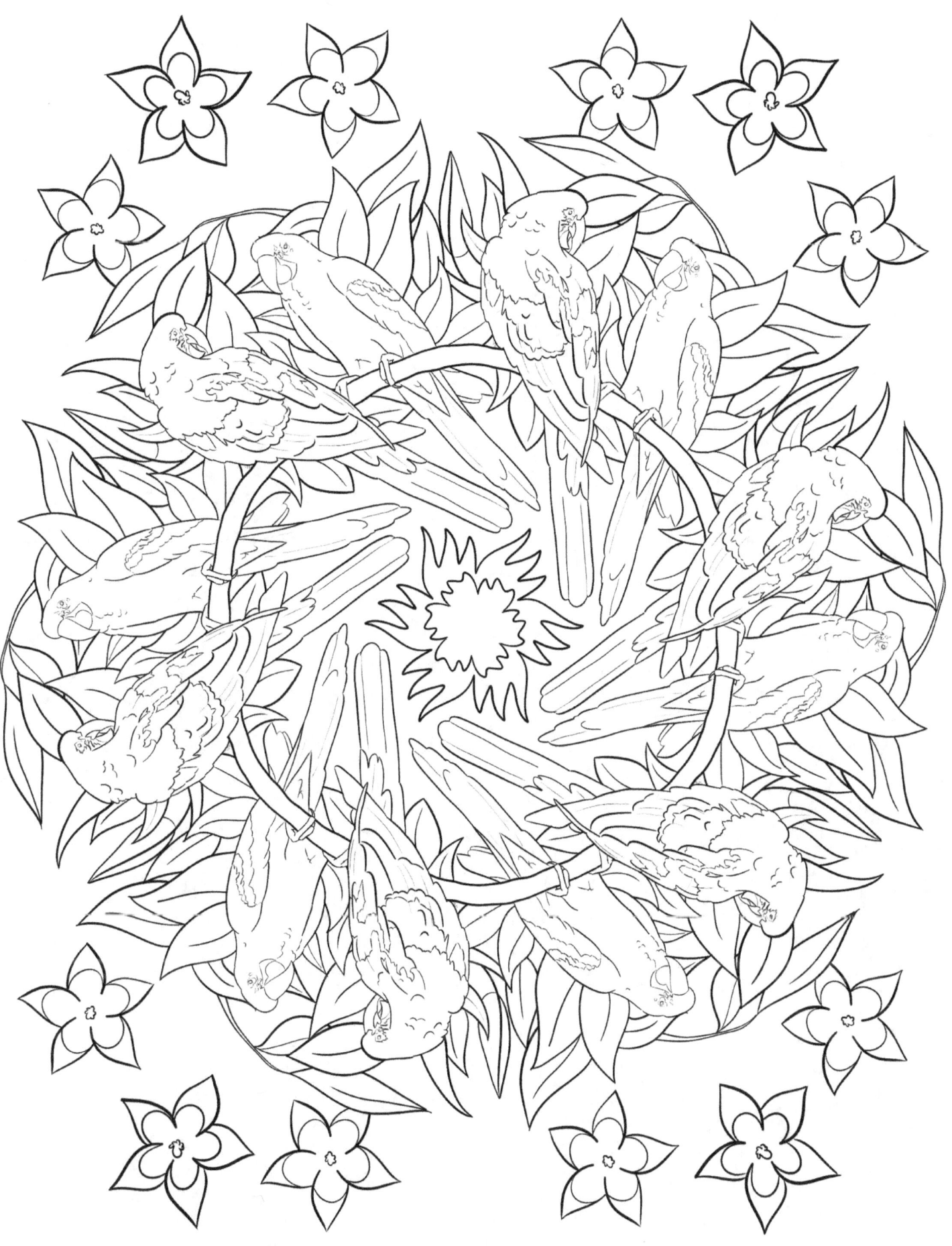

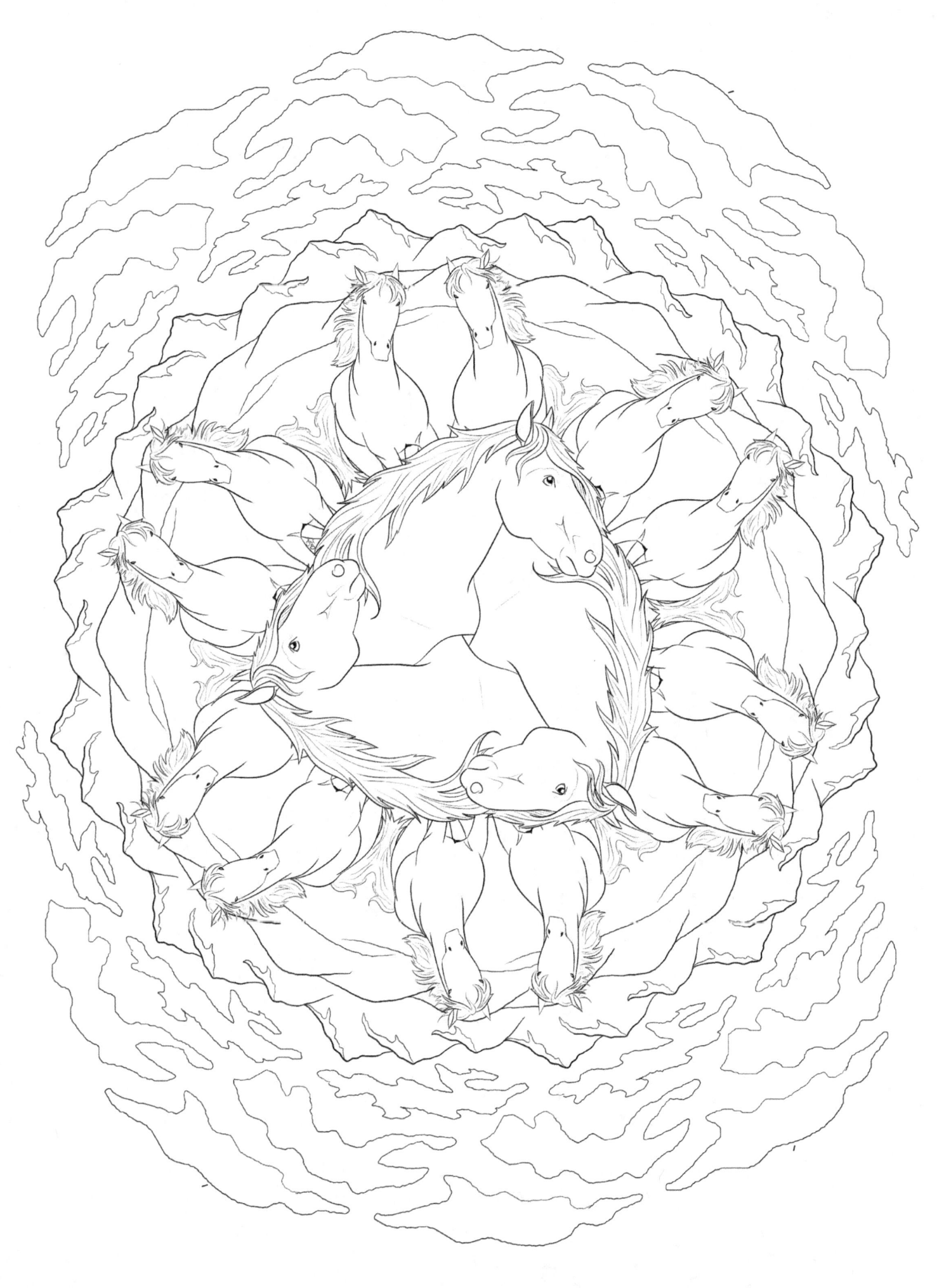

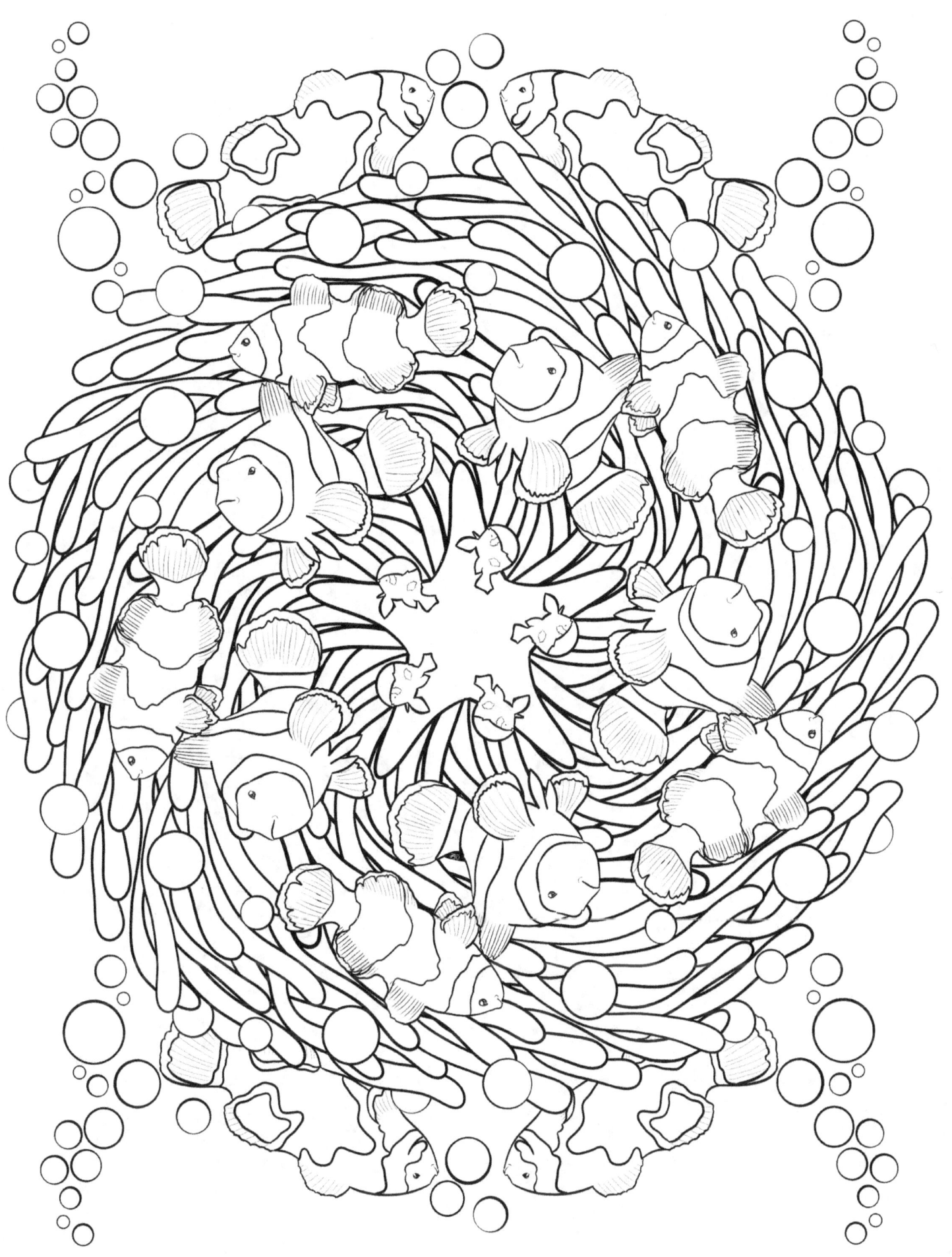

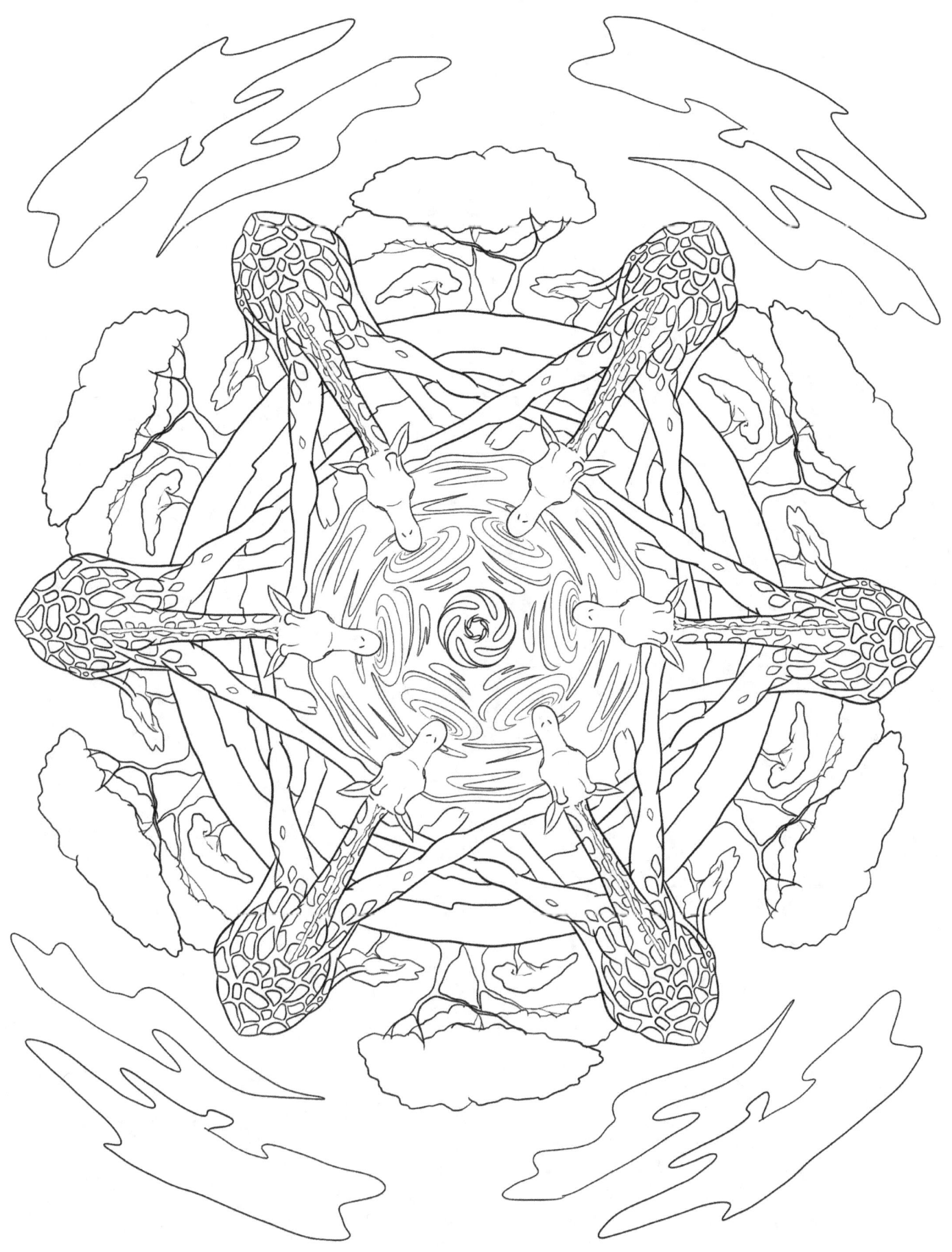

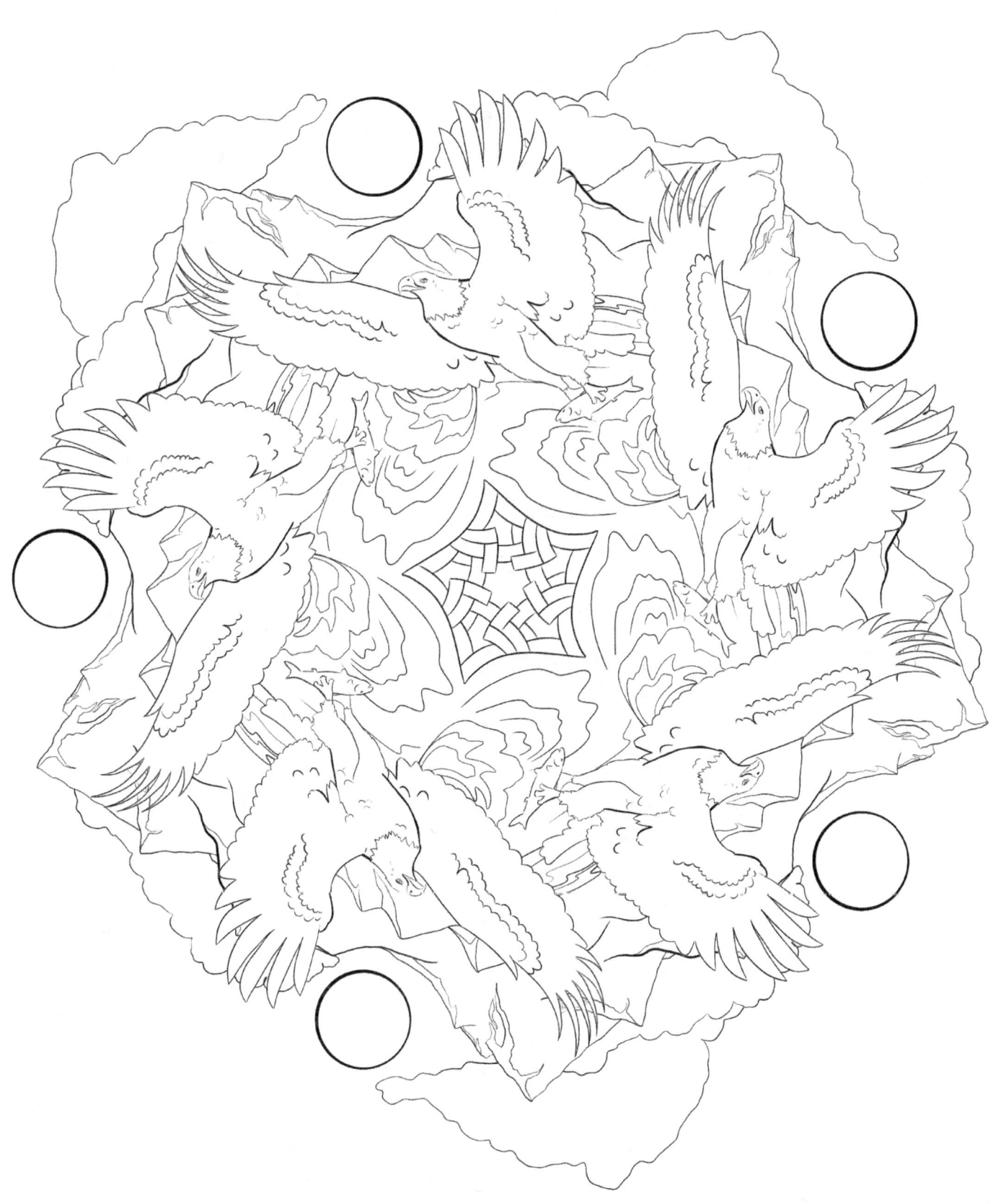

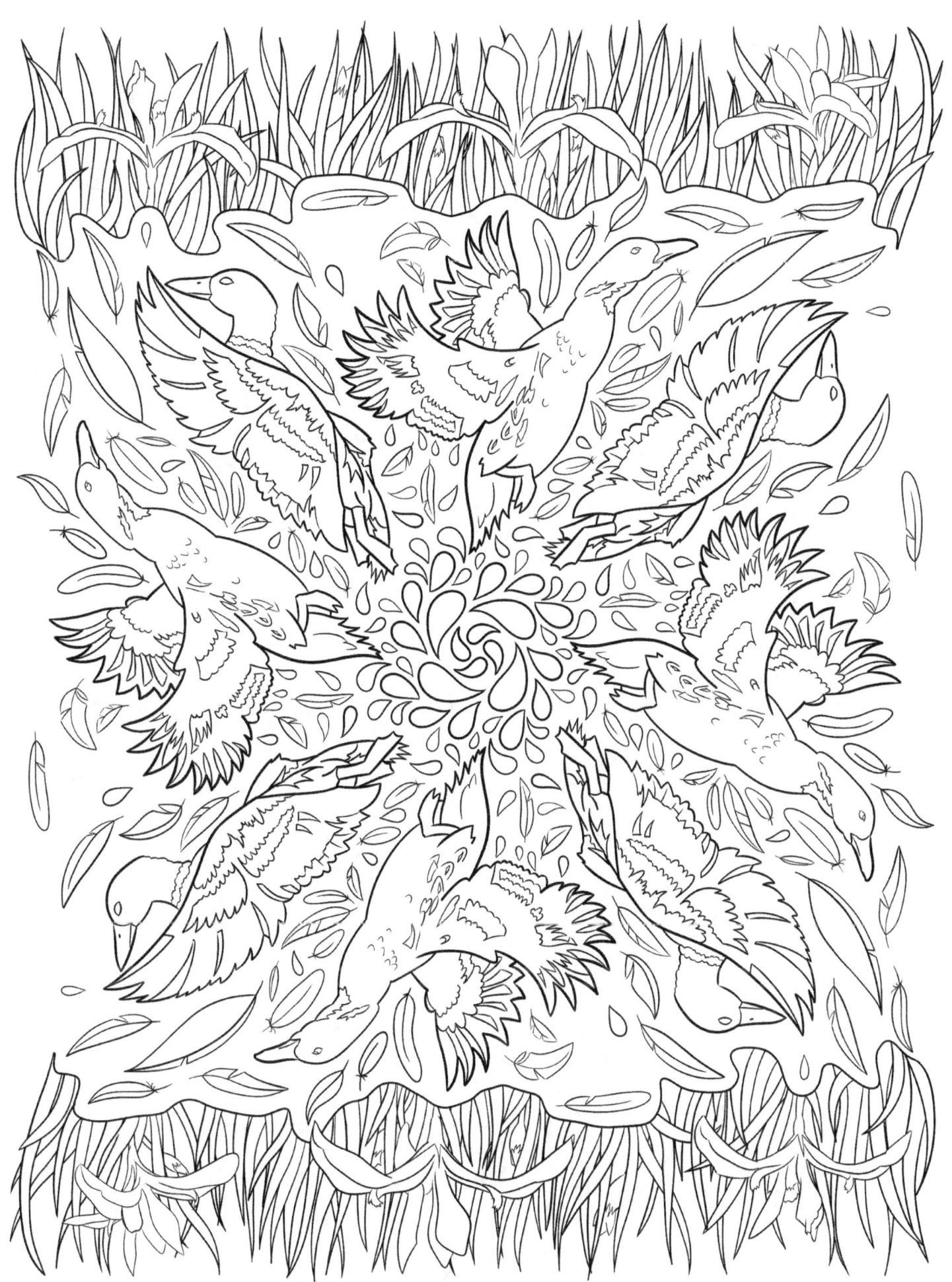

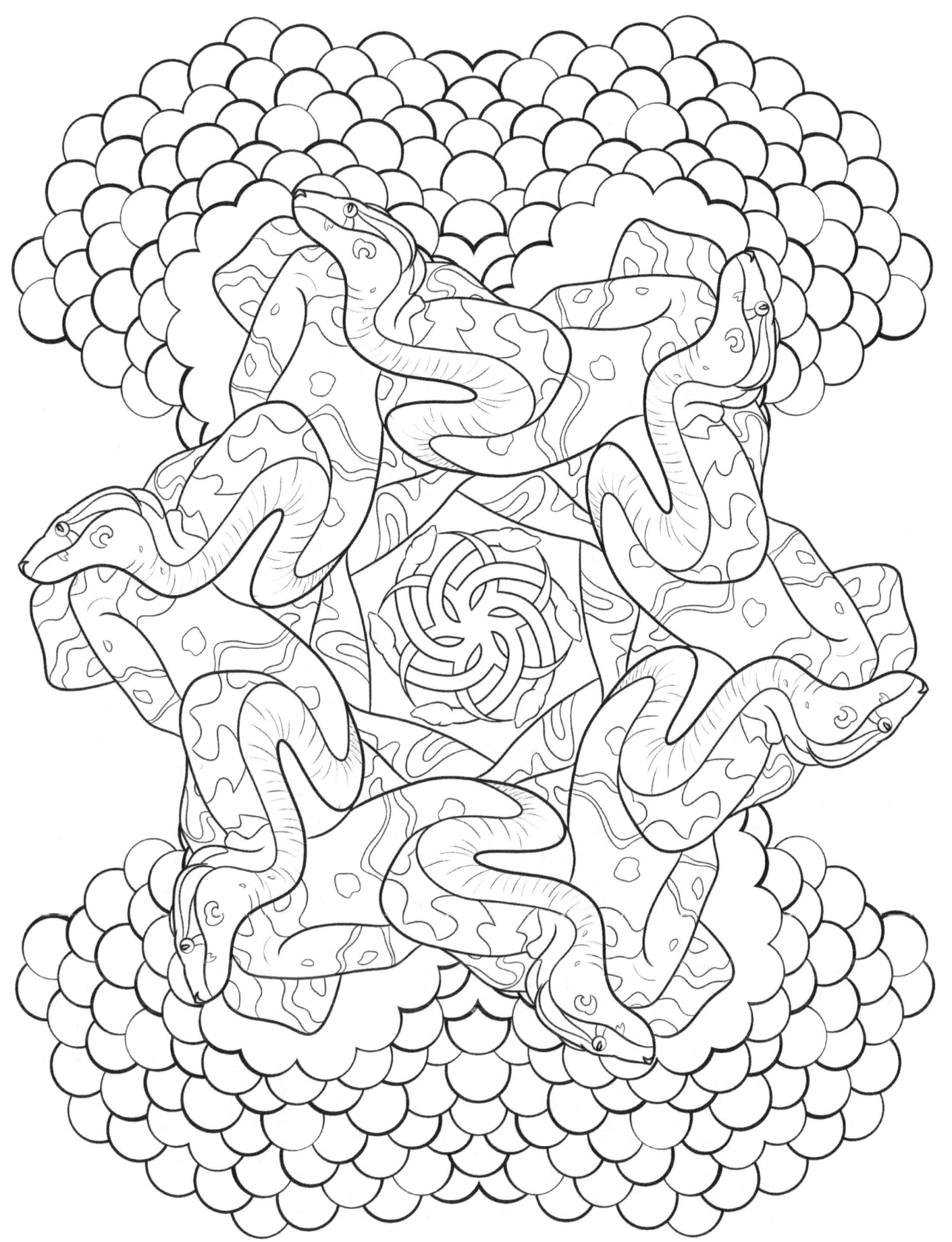

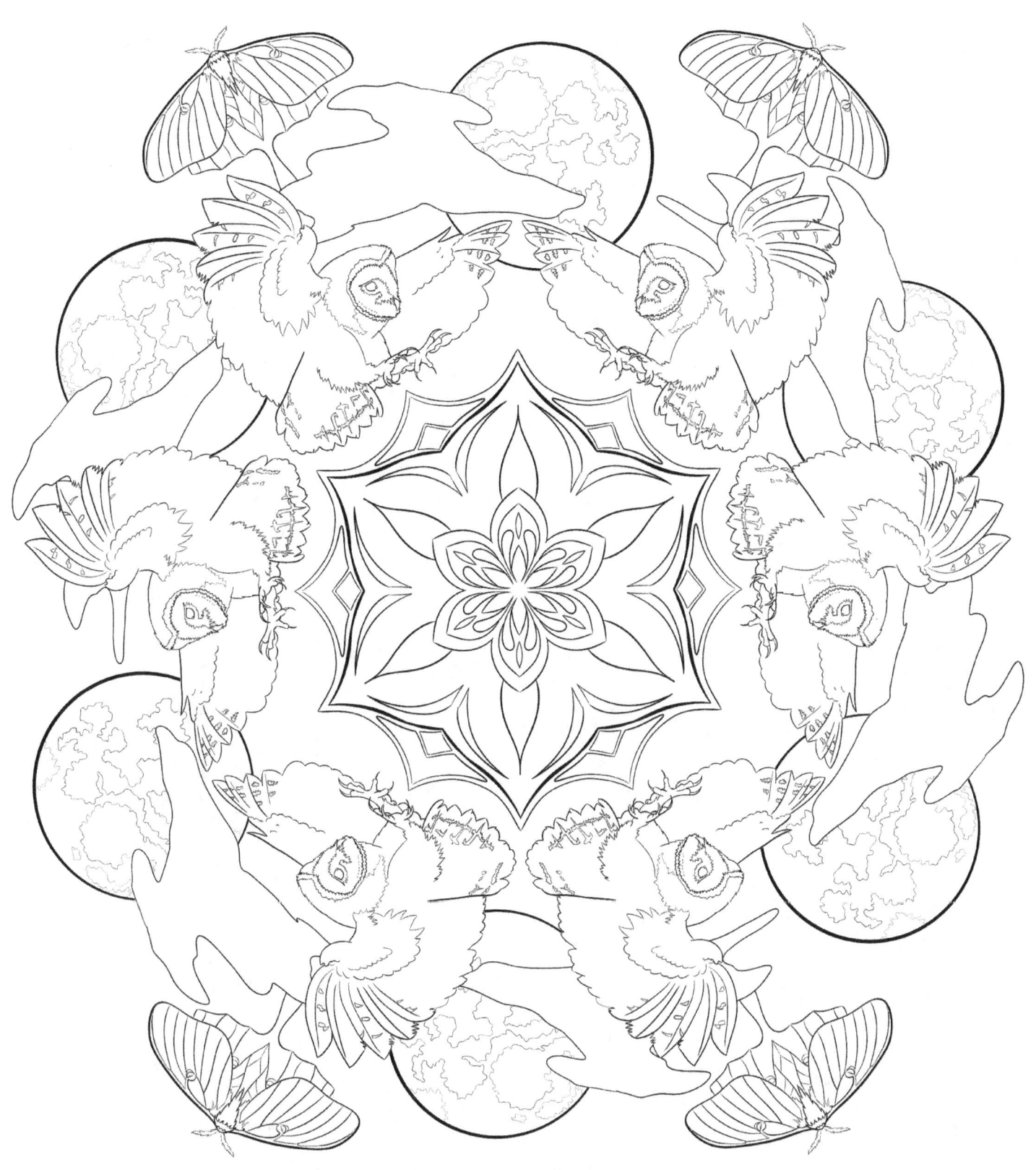

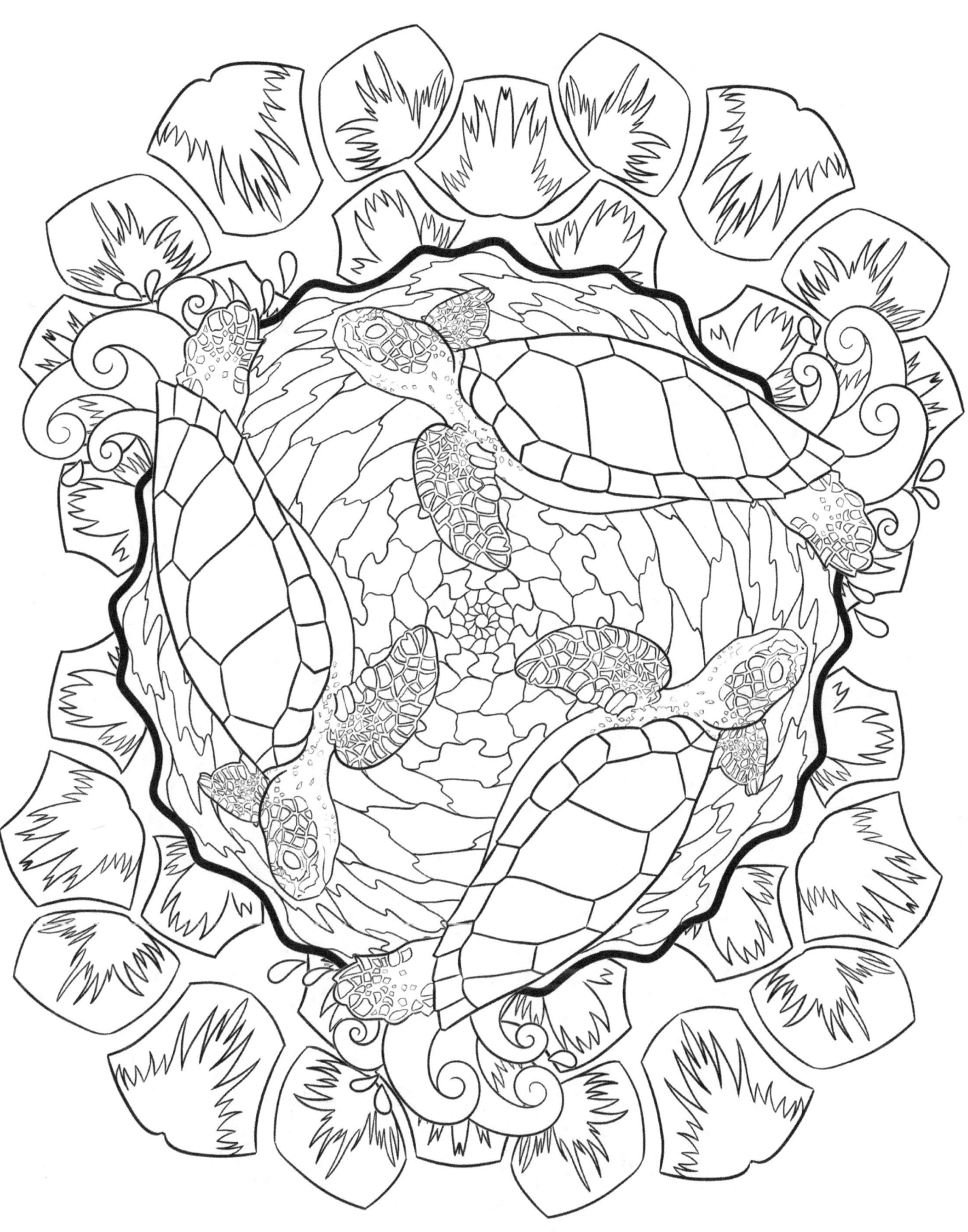

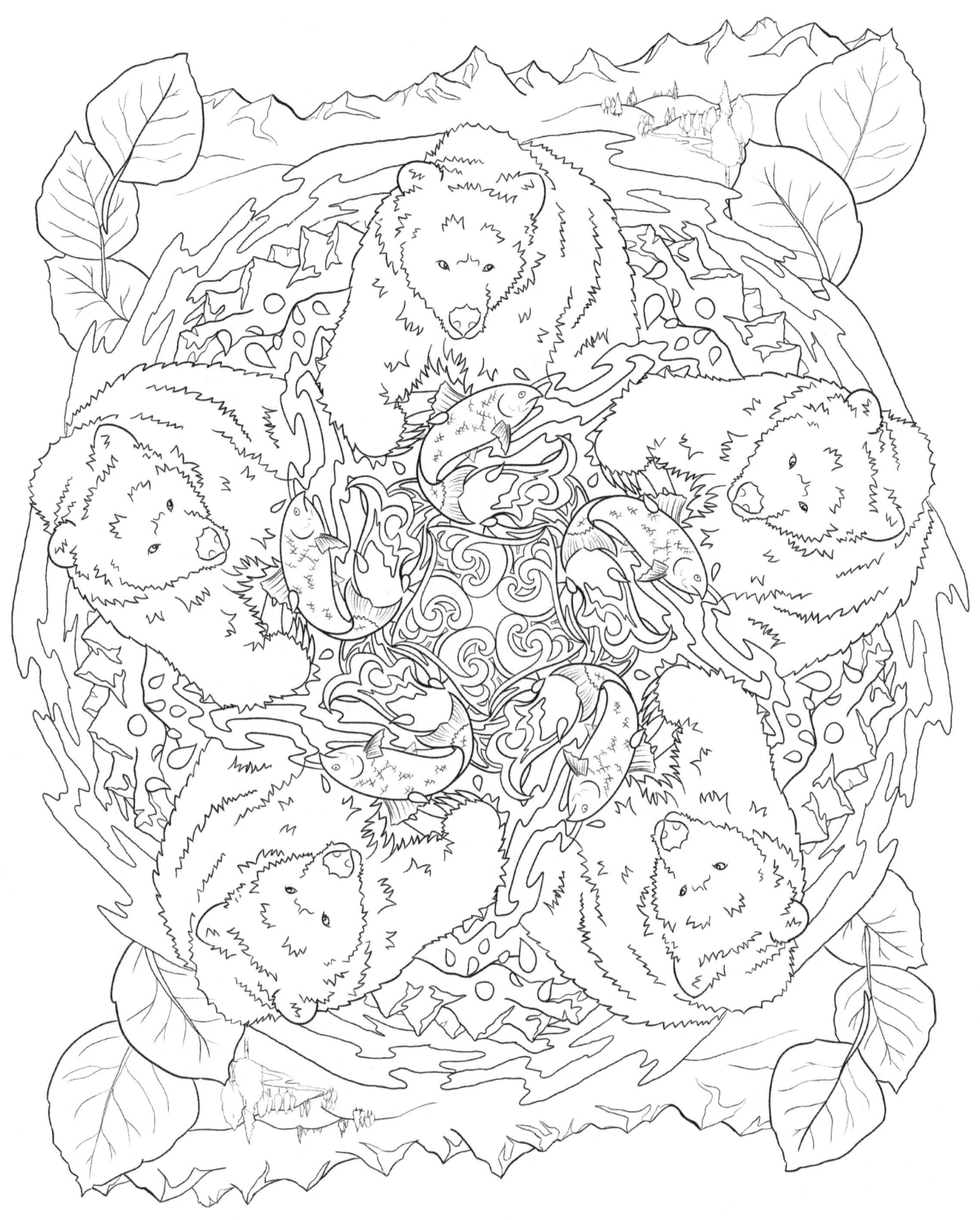

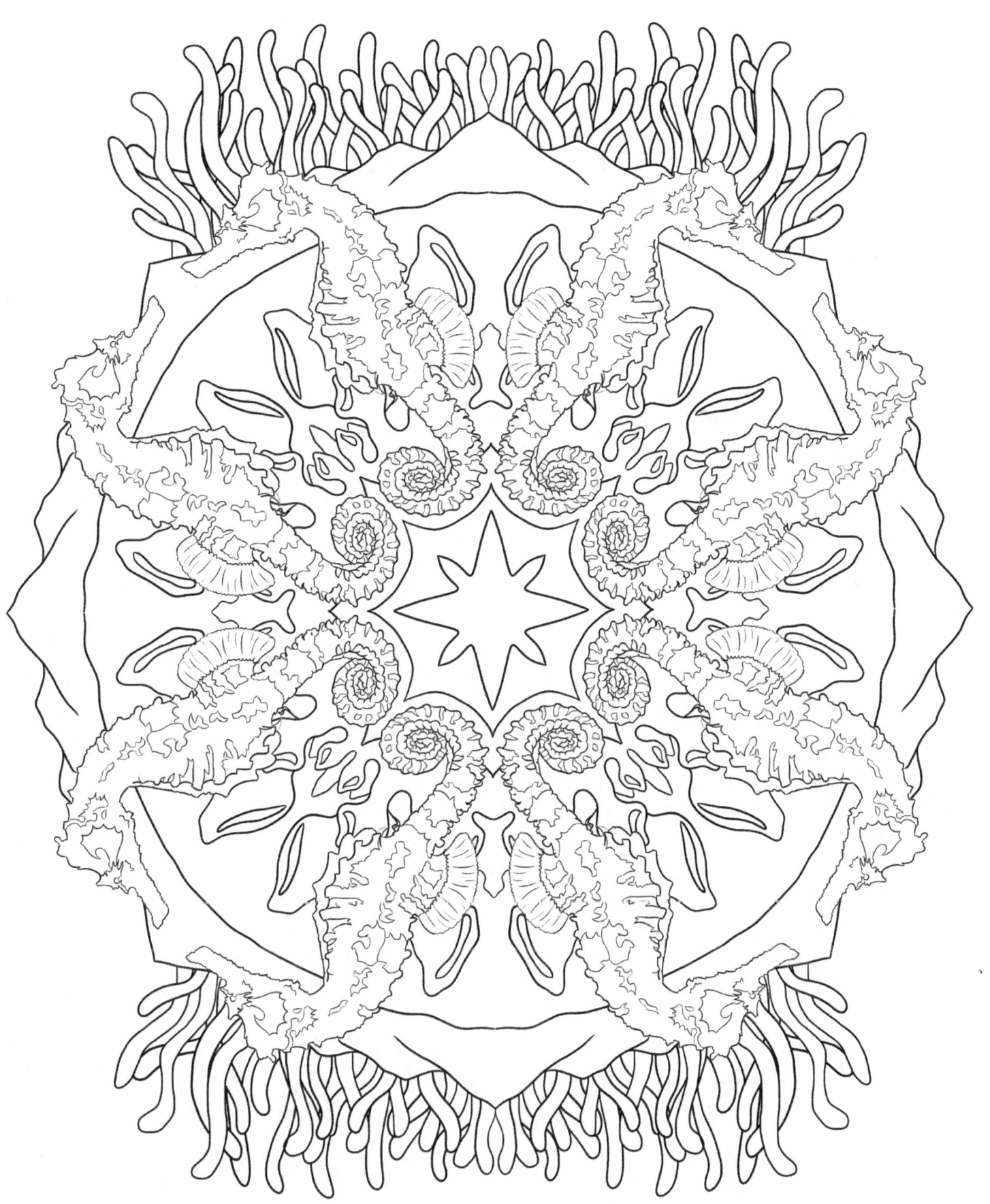

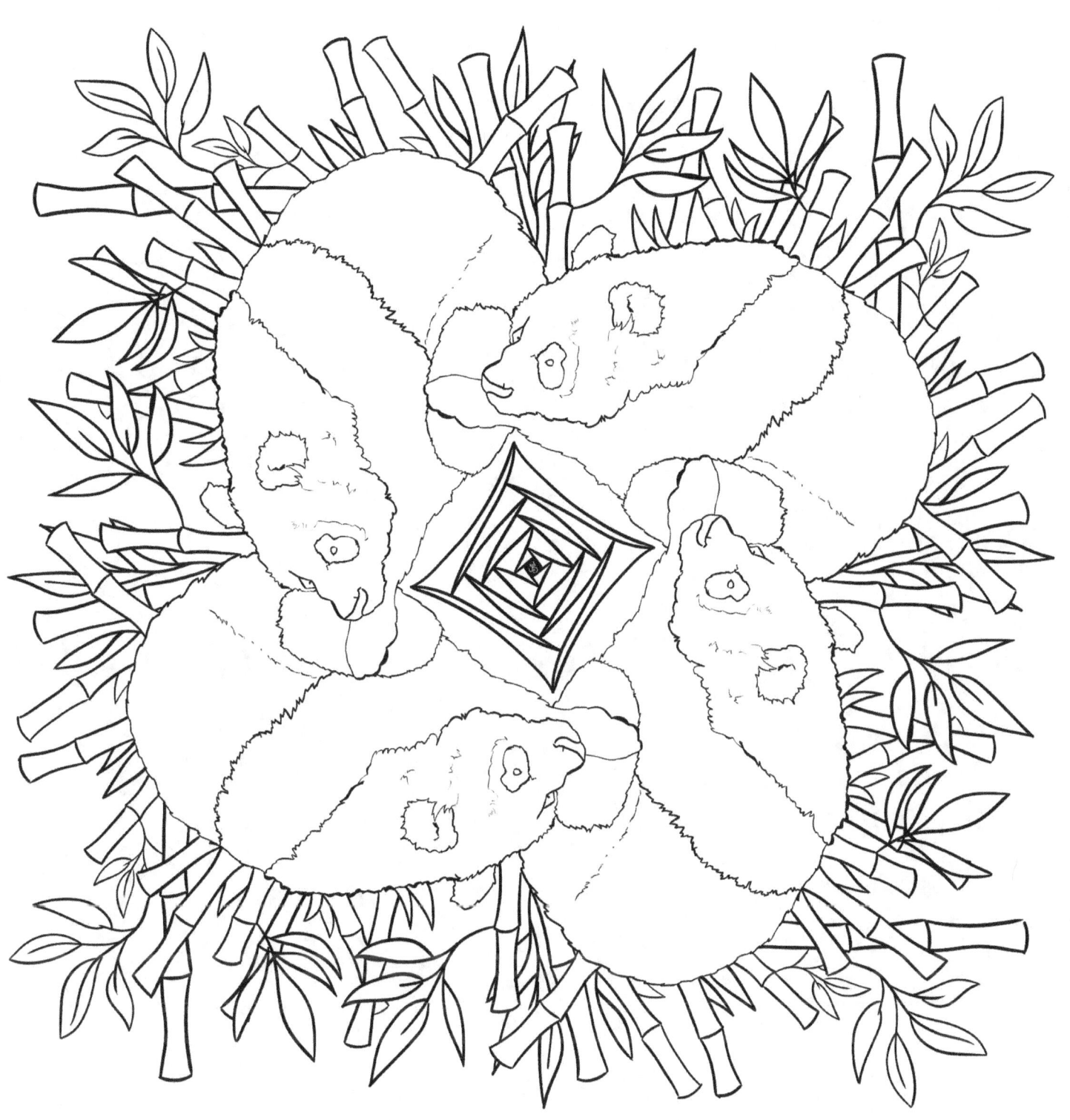

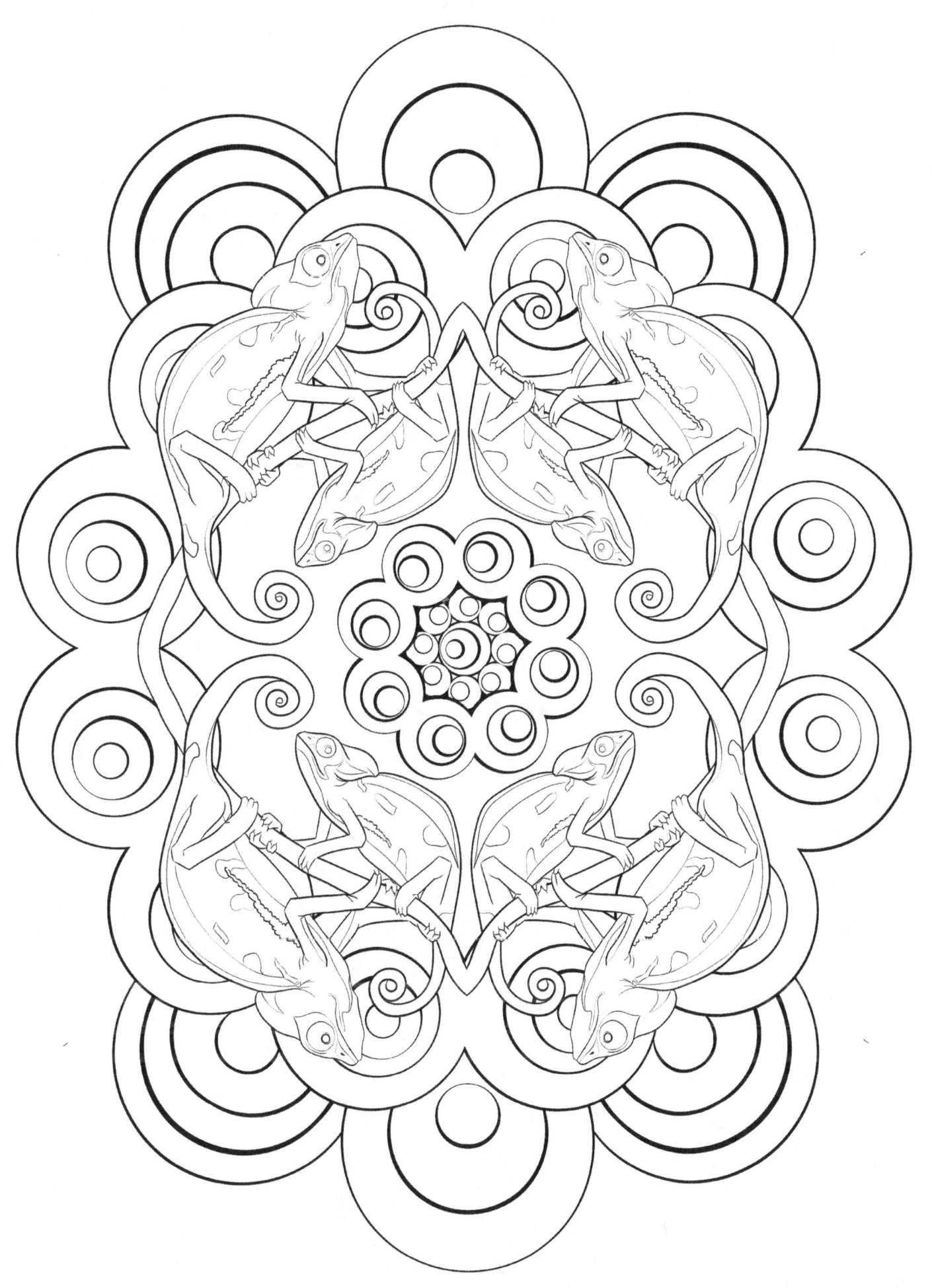

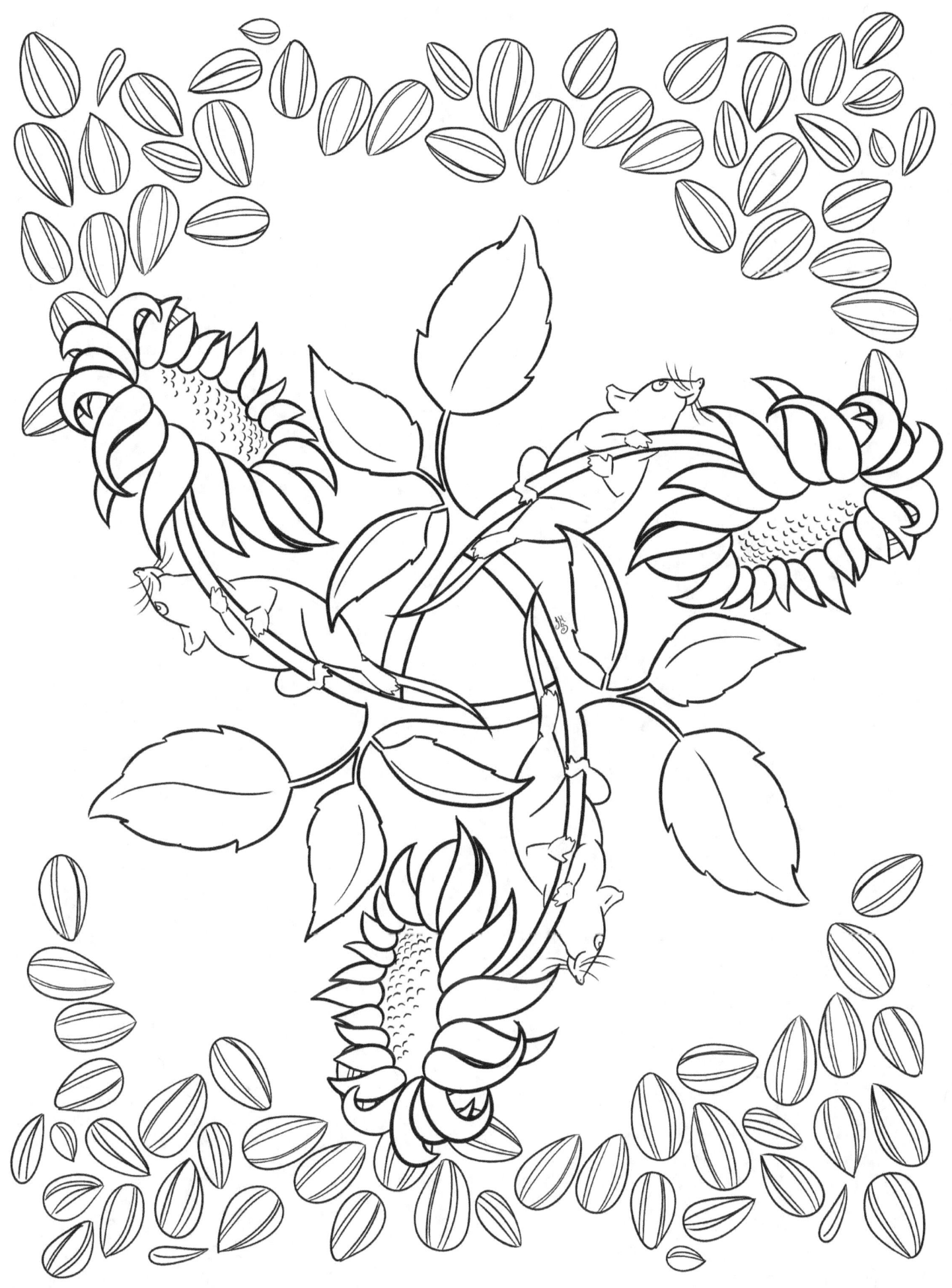

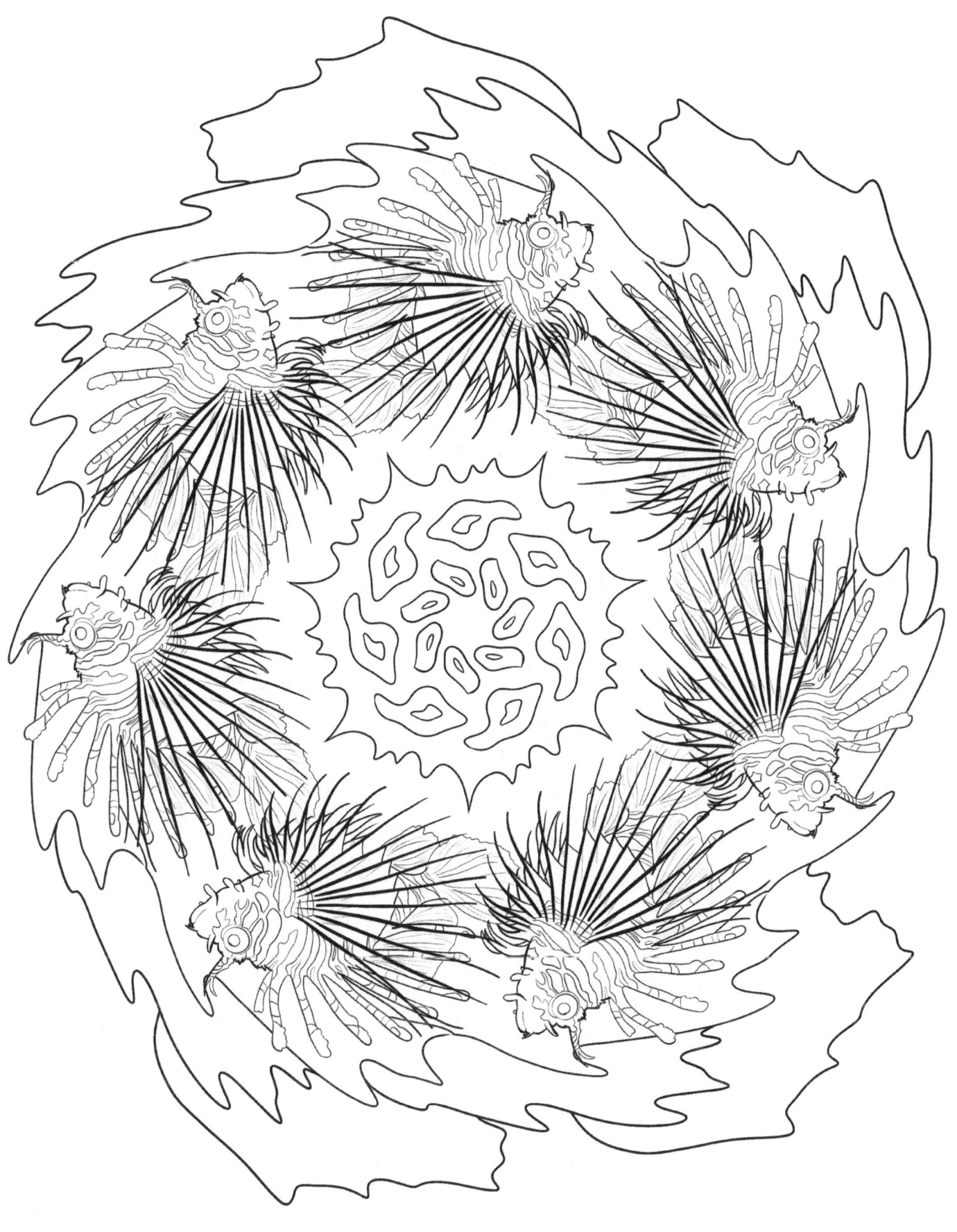

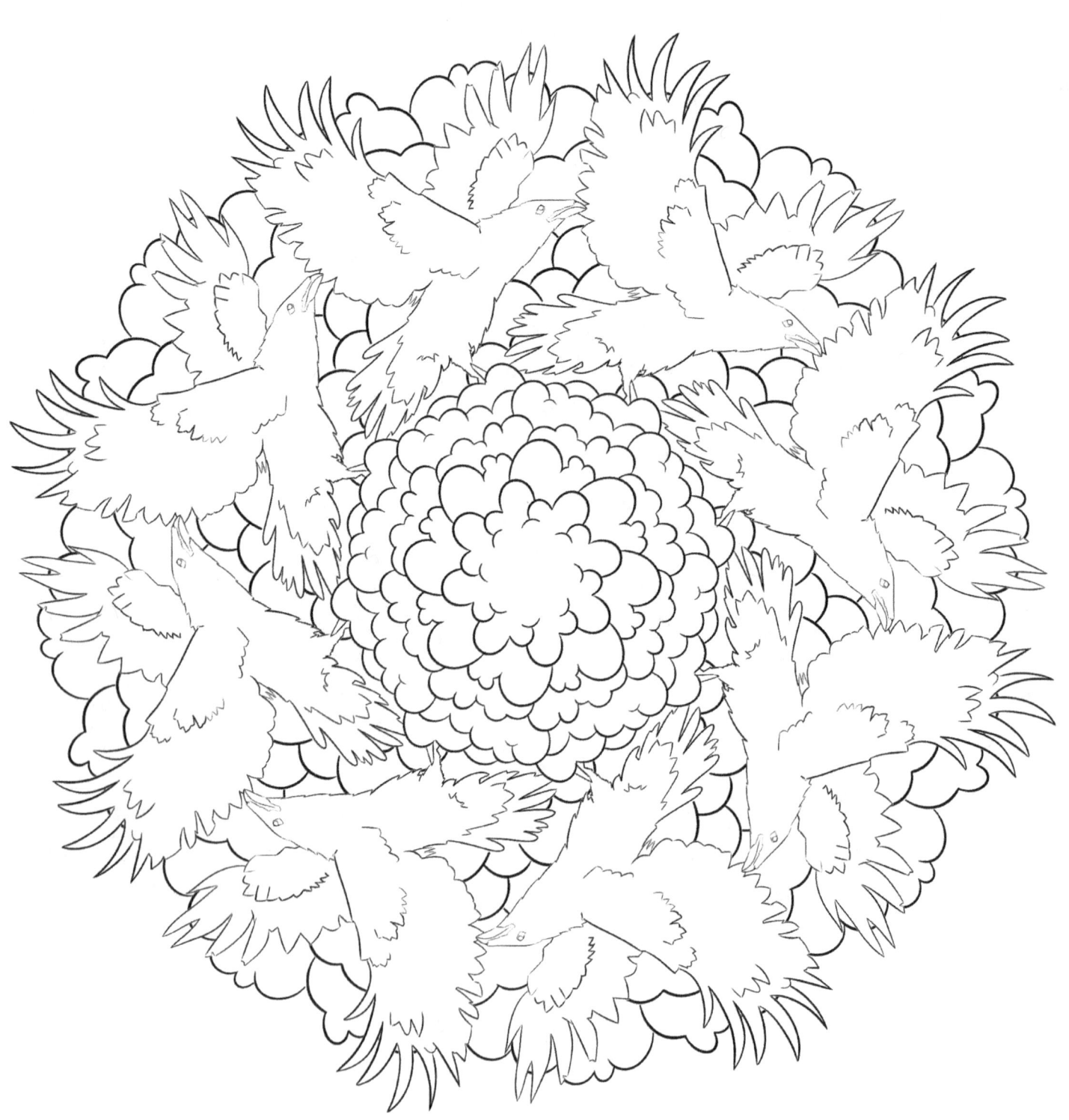

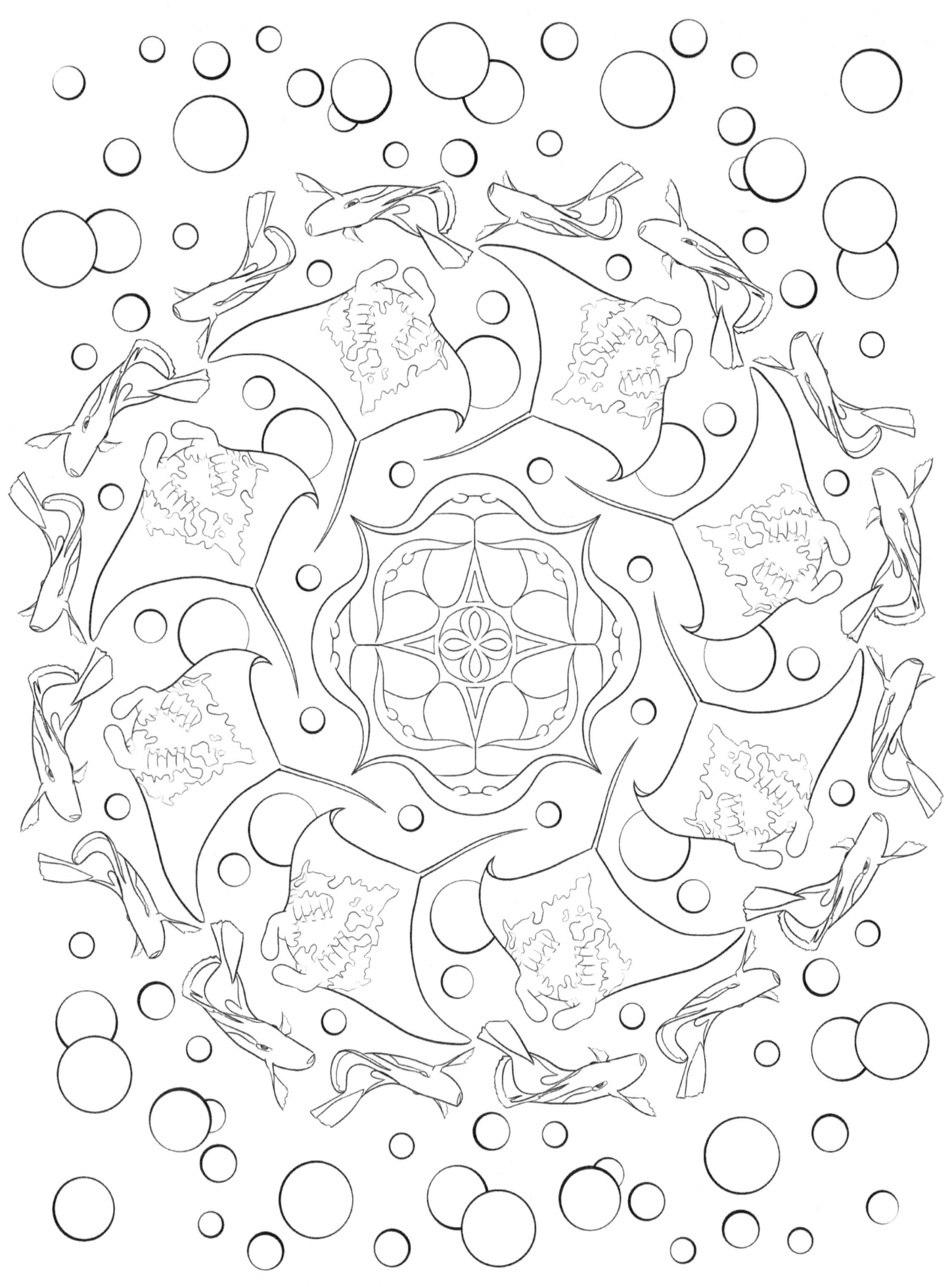

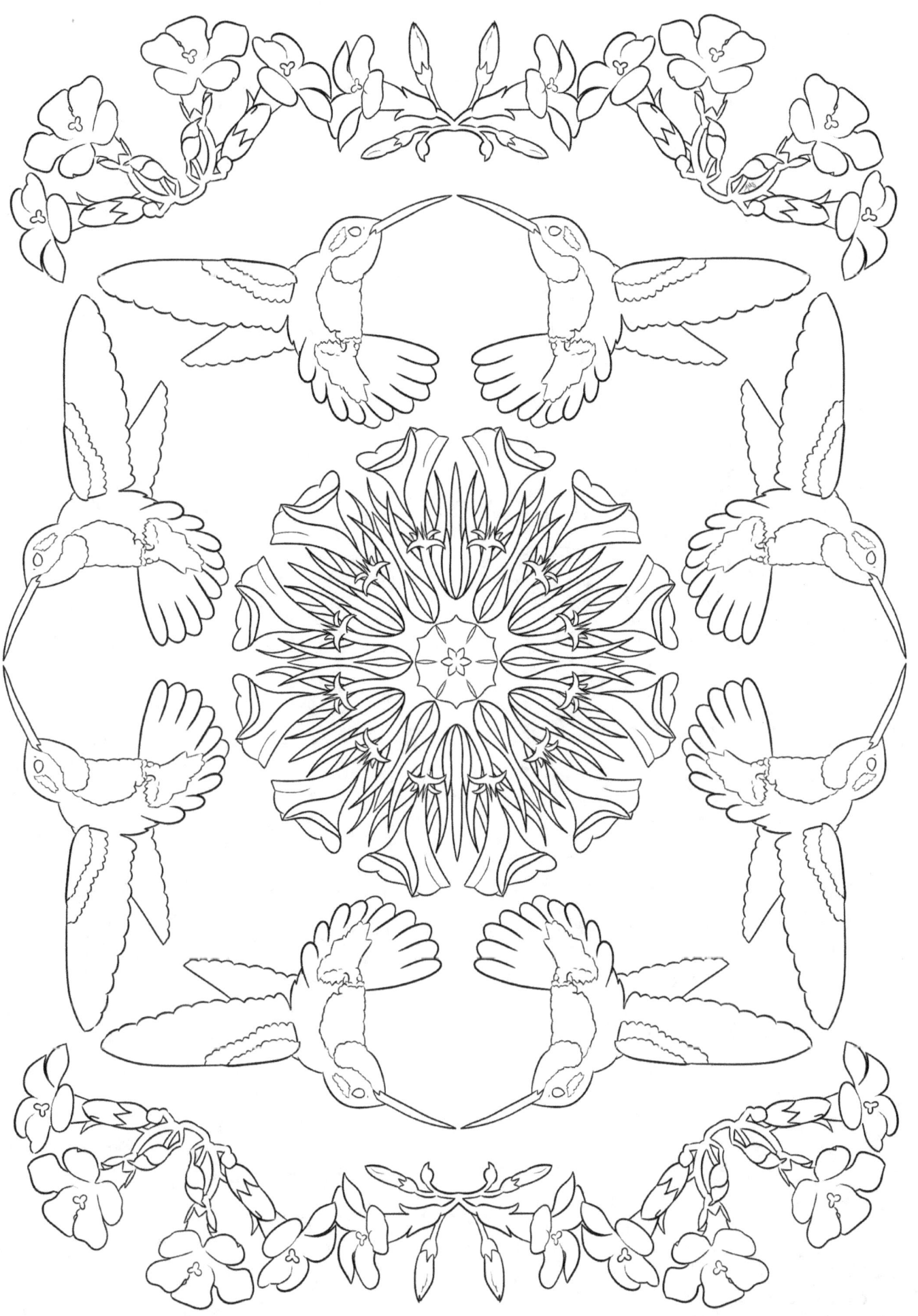

www.ingramcontent.com/pod-product-compliance
Lightning Source LLC
Chambersburg PA
CBHW080133240526
45468CB00009BA/2401